Shortcuts to Mindfulness

100 Ways to Personal and Spiritual Growth

Catherine Auman, LMFT

Green Tara Press

Los Angeles

2014

Green Tara Press
Los Angeles, CA 90064
www.greentarapress.com

Some of the essays in the collection previously appeared in the
following: "Simple Cures for Loneliness" and "Sunshine In a Box in
Spirituality and Health, "The Sacred Prostitute in the Ancient World"
is an abbreviated version of a longer piece published in *The Mountain
Astrologer, AstroLogos,* and *Zodiac,* and "Is There Such a Thing as Sex
Addiction" in *Spotlight on Recovery.* Many of these essays appeared
online on *sex.com, ezinearticles.com, selfgrowth.com,* and other sites.
"The Roots of Tantra, Parts One and Two" are excerpts from Catherine Auman's novel, *blissbody.*

Library of Congress In-Publication Data

Auman, Catherine I.
Shortcuts to Mindfulness: 100 Ways to Personal and Spiritual Growth
1. Psychology 2. Spirituality 3. Self Help

ISBN 978-0-9898305-3-9 (paperback)
ISBN 978-0-9898305-4-6 (electronic book text)

Cover and interior book design by
Lilly Penhall, Interstellar Graphics
www.interstellargraphics.com

More Praise for Catherine Auman

"Catherine Auman's intelligent work inspires my heart and mind and echoes with her profound humanity. With astute psychological and spiritual wisdom, she addresses the practical issues that we encounter on the path of awakening. Whenever I read her writing, I feel grateful and happy that people can learn and practice with such a trustworthy guide."

— Trudy Goodman, Ph.D., Senior Vipassana teacher and Founder of InsightLA

"Catherine Auman has written an important book that I will read more than once. The psychological teachings are eye opening and are weaved in with nuanced spiritual wisdom. Her writings help me to appreciate a new perspective. She is a wonderful teacher. If I were ever going to begin psychotherapy again, I would choose Ms. Auman as my therapist. This book should be required reading for all those hoping to attain better mental health and spiritual development!"

— Alan Gettis, Ph.D., author of *It's All Part of the Dance: Finding Happiness in an Upside Down World*

"Catherine Auman's writings resonate with me regarding things I've been feeling, contemplating, and experiencing. I printed out one piece and gave it to several clients today, and used another during the meditations I facilitate. I have posted several of her pieces to my website for inspired readings for my students, clients, family and friends. I love the wisdom that Catherine offers; her writings always bring me back to a more humbled, in-tune and spiritually-connected place."

— Sara Lederer, Psy.D., Licensed Psychologist and Professor at Argosy University

"Catherine Auman is one of the most brilliant and inspiring leading-edge psychotherapists that I've had the pleasure to meet. Her insights are down-to-earth, thought-provoking, and life-changing. I love to share Catherine's amazing essays with my clients, as I know each one of them will be transformative and impactful."

— Saida Désilets, Ph.D., author of *Emergence of the Sensual Woman*

For You. You Know Who You Are.

Contents

Introduction

Sex.com was on the phone. They had found me by Internet search and wanted to offer me a position as a paid columnist. The new owner's vision was to turn *sex.com* into the destination site for all things sexual: not only porn but sex facts and information, products, toys, books, and expert advice. They wanted to recruit a reputable, licensed professional. I came to their attention because of my resume and my adventures studying tantra.

My column "Everyday Ecstasy" ran for nine months, during which time many of these articles were written. Abruptly, the gig ended as the owner gave up his lofty intentions and returned to all-porn, realizing, I suppose, that there was no money in an all-purpose sex information site. But I had become hooked on the short format and began turning out articles on other subjects I hoped others would find useful.

Some of these articles were written for *sex.com*. Others are teaching stories I share in psychotherapy sessions with clients. Several have been published in national magazines. All have been posted on Facebook, and many are on sites all over the web. At last count, my free articles online have been read by over 14,000 readers, and I hope many more will find help from them as the years progress.

It has always been my intention that when I had 100 short articles, I would publish a collection. Here they are. I have tried to present interesting topics concise enough for the modern attention span: something to read at the car wash, on the metro, or while waiting for a friend to text you back. I hope you will be amused, educated, enlivened, and awakened.

In love and service,

Catherine Auman

Chapter 1

It Takes A Strong Vase To Hold The Water

Personal Growth and the Ostrich Egg

It was hot that summer, hotter than four kids from the chilly Pacific Northwest could comprehend. Our dad had gotten a math scholarship for six weeks in Champaign-Urbana, Illinois, so he and Mom had piled all us kids into the Volkswagen van and headed off cross country to a planet very unlike our own.

It was way too hot to play outside, so every day we escaped to the air-conditioned shopping center across the street. Malls were not yet ubiquitous, seemed jammed full of mystical treasures, and our parents let us go over unchaperoned!—the immensity of this freedom was almost inconceivable to us.

The most magical treat of all was right inside the front door: an aquarium that held six chicken eggs and a gigantic four-pounder from an ostrich. Listed on the pedestal below were the dates they were expected to hatch. It was only a matter of weeks, but in the time frame of children, forever. We waited every single day that summer for those eggs to hatch, and every single day we would run over to the mall to see if it was time yet. Waiting, waiting, we waited—and not too patiently.

The ostrich egg turned out to be a dud. But every one of us, my brother and sisters and I, remember the best day of the summer as the one when we arrived and the chickens were

19

finally hatching. We city kids watched the natural miracle as they pecked their way out of their shells, wet and squeaking. We found out it wasn't all sanitized, Disney-fied as we'd been led to expect by the cartoons where adorable baby chicks burst out of their shells spotless and downy. It took untold effort for them to facilitate their own births, and one chick was bloody from being cut by its shell.

I often recount this story for my patients who are grappling with why it all hurts so much. The way of personal and spiritual growth takes untold effort and is often "bloody." It doesn't just spring out fully formed because you say a few affirmations or read shelves of self-help books. It's a painful process; there are no two ways about it. "Your pain is the breaking of the shell that encloses your understanding," Kahlil Gibran wrote. Just as in the birth process of the chicks, the pain and struggle involved in the birthing of oneself is not an aberration, but the most natural thing in the world.

Feeling More Alive While You're Alive

Some spiritual seekers are wan and dull and gray. They haven't committed to being fully alive in their bodies, and their interest in spirituality becomes a way to avoid being so. There is no reason spiritual people can't be the most vitally alive people on the planet. Increasing a sense of aliveness has to do with allowing more energy into the body and releasing blocks that keep energy trapped.

Forbes magazine recently featured Richard Branson, the adventurer, entrepreneur, and founder of Virgin Airlines. Now in his late 60s, he has started a new travel company for outer space, continues his sailboat racing, and spends 70% of his time on philanthropy. When asked for advice on how to increase energy, he responded, "Work out more." Working out gives him at least four hours of additional productive time a day, he said.

It seems counterintuitive that we would gain energy by expending energy, but in the case of vigorous exercise, that's the case. Athletic training improves metabolic efficiency, blood circulation, and general fitness so that more energy is available.

In addition to exercise, there are somatic disciplines that make available energy that is trapped in the body by promoting relaxation and reducing chronic tension. Weight training is an example, as are various bodywork therapies: Rolfing, Polarity, the Alexander technique, breathing practices, and massage of all types.

Taking care of our bodies includes proper nutrition. Many of the foods we eat today do not promote vitality. If we are not eating right, we will not feel alive. The key is to eat as many fresh vegetables and fruit as possible.

Psychotherapy can release energy that is being used to suppress our feelings, keep a lid on our inner life, and deny our reality. When therapy is successful, it lifts repressions, unblocks defenses against strong feeling and resolves internal conflicts, infusing a whole new energetic response to life.

Each person has his or her own unique sources of vitality, and it's helpful to identify them. What kind of music do we find enlivening? What kind of books, TV shows; which friends? We can look back at certain periods of our lives when we felt particularly alive to discover what habits and disciplines could be incorporated today. As much as possible, we can strive to practice the disciplines of vitality in order to be alive as we can for as long as we are alive.

It's Simple: Breathe Deep, Feel Good

I first began thinking about oxygen back when I started a running program (it was a milestone birthday and I realized, "Damn, I've got to get in shape!"). I'd been walking about an hour a day for years after hearing that exercise was the most effective treatment for depression. Walking had helped, but when I began running, my mood spiked up in a way that made me realize it hadn't been enough. I ran my one and only 5K at the completion of the program and then promptly went back to walking. The running since then is sporadic, but the times when I do, my mood seems to match the level of oxygen consumed.

When we breathe, we can feel our feelings, both pleasurable and difficult. In this culture, however, we are taught to do whatever we can to avoid feeling bad. Anything unpleasant, and we are expected to will it away, or dispense of it through alcohol, food, or positive thinking. Holding one's breath is quite effective at stopping feelings. It works.

People often hold their breath when faced with something uncomfortable. It can be as simple as encountering a driver with road rage, to as complex as trauma from childhood abuse. But habitually stopping one's feelings can become a chronic pattern of which a person is entirely unaware. Chronic

23

holding means that some of us never take a full, deep breath anymore. Tension is locked in the body anywhere that breath will not go.

Leonard Orr's Rebirthing and Stan Grof's Holotropic Breathwork are two techniques that involve having the client relax in the presence of a coach or partner and begin to take full deep breaths. This can induce all kinds of effects: recall of traumatic events, muscle contractions, crying and screaming, streaming bliss states. Orr believed that a basic series of ten sessions would be enough to "unlock" the breath and create profound and lasting change.

When emotions are released that were previously stopped with the breath, there is often a corresponding release of vitality. It takes a lot of energy to keep those emotions repressed in the body.

The yogis have left us many breathing techniques for optimum health and wellbeing. Tantrikas, yogis, and energy healers use the breath to process out old, stuck emotions and induce higher states of consciousness. In my practice, I often teach my patients how an anxious, unhappy breath is shallow and rapid, filling only the top part of the lungs. Together we will practice a relaxed breath, deep and slow and full into the belly.

So go ahead, take a nice deep, slow inhale, bringing the breath all the way down to your tailbone. Now, let it out slowly, then slower still. Who knew feeling blissful was this easy? Or that it is available at every moment, every day of your life.

Monkey See, Monkey Do

The pain in their eyes is chilling. The baby monkeys cling desperately to their mothers-made-of-wire for up to eighteen hours a day. They barely have appetite for food; they are starving for affection and warmth. If you search YouTube for "Harlow monkeys," you can view the old videos from the 50s and see what I mean.

When Dr. Harry Harlow began his work in the 1930s, he set out to conduct experiments on the nature of love. Child rearing practices of the time maintained that too much physical touch would spoil children. Dr. Harlow's research was controversial, but at least that harmful theory was discarded.

Dr. Harlow created "mothers" out of wire and wood. Some were wrapped in terry cloth while the others were left as bare wire. The baby monkeys clung for comfort to the cloth mothers, and even when the wire mothers were equipped to feed the babies, the infants still preferred to cuddle against the soft terry cloth. Harlow concluded that "contact comfort" was essential to the psychological health of infant monkeys and children. He also believed that either fathers or mothers could provide this comfort, which was a revolutionary idea at the time.

The animal liberation movement was begun as a protest against these experiments, and critics don't see them as having anything to do with love. Dr. Harlow defended his research by saying, "What do we mean that a child loves its mother? We mean that he experiences a great feeling of security in her presence, and when frightened he runs to his mother to touch her to drive away his fears. This contact with the mother changes his entire personality."

I saw these monkey experiments at the Seattle World's Fair when I wasn't much more than an infant myself. I can still feel the heartbreak when I remember the babies trying to get love from such impoverished mothers, or when I re-watch the videos. It makes me consider all the people who go through life having only had "wire mothers (fathers)" who are desperately craving the warmth we mammals need to survive. In my practice, I see many people who didn't get enough "contact comfort" in childhood, and this lack of love has damaged their lives.

We are living in a culture where an increasing number of people are suffering from loneliness and lack of human touch. Humans (and monkeys) can actually die for want of love, of warmth and cuddling. Harry Harlow's research "demonstrated the importance of care-giving and companionship in social and cognitive development," but what it means for us is that we all need to give each other more touch. As we see monkeys do, we need to do: admit how much we need it and offer each other the comfort of our contact.

"Get Busy Living or Get Busy Dying"

This quote from *The Shawshank Redemption* keeps Gary Bowsher climbing mountains, both literally and figuratively, even though he has Parkinson's Disease.

Shortly after his diagnosis in 2007 at the age of 52, Gary read a newspaper article about "The Top Ten Fire Lookout Hikes in the Pacific Northwest." So far, he has checked-off eight of them, including the ones on Pilchuk, Granite, Baker, and two on Mount Rainier. He may not be the fastest walker on the trail, and sometimes he needs a helping hand but, "my feeling is that you need to keep moving, even if it hurts," he said. "I'm going to live every year as if it's my last." In that spirit, Gary flew down to walk seven miles of the LA Marathon with his sister to make sure she completed the race.

Parkinson's Disease (PD) is a degenerative disorder of the nervous system with no known cause and no cure, as of yet. The prognosis for PD sufferers is not good as the disease inevitably progresses with time and causes a lessened life expectancy. The best hope for people with PD lies in the ongoing research efforts. Michael J. Fox, who has had PD since 1991, has raised both awareness and lots of money for the cause. "Hope is very important," as Gary says.

Gary has never exhibited the shaking or tremors that most of us think of as Parkinson's; rather, his symptoms are stiffness, rigidity, and difficulties with walking and sleep. The onset was insidious: Gary was enjoying a stroll with his father-in-law, happily oblivious to the fact that anything was wrong until it was pointed out that his right arm wasn't swinging when he walked. Gary then started noticing that he couldn't shave or brush his teeth with that hand either, and over time the other symptoms revealed themselves.

Although there is no cure for PD, very good medications are available that provide symptom relief, and doctors often prescribe supplements such as antioxidants. Gary eats as many fruits and vegetables as he can, although he is especially famous for ordering apple pie as his first course in a restaurant. Regular exercise is recommended, hence Gary's walking regime.

Just as Michael J. Fox's dignity and activism in the face of his disease have inspired so many, so has Gary's "Just Do It!" attitude. Gary's continued optimism, zest for life, and love for his family are daily miracles. That he is an inspiration to everyone around him I can personally attest to, because Gary Bowsher is my brother.

Innies and Outies

I used to feel bad about being an introvert. It's just really supremely nerdy to prefer to stay home and read. I was born that way, though, what can I say? Even when I was little, I remember my mother yelling at me, "Cathy, stop reading and go outside and play." In a minute, Mom, in a minute. After I finish this paragraph, this chapter, this 800-page book.

America is an extravagantly extroverted culture. People are judged on their social skills, their level of apparent happiness and "positivity," and their lack of thinking deeply. Other cultures, such as Asian ones, do not particularly value extroversion, and introverted people don't feel as ostracized as we do here.

Someone once defined the difference this way: extroverts reach out to other people for stress relief while introverts prefer to be alone. This is only partially true, as everyone gets a mood boost from the company of others; rather, it is the number of people to whom one turns. Extroverts love hanging out in groups; introverts prefer meeting one-on-one with close friends.

While extroverts are partying down, introverts prefer less stimulus and more time for listening and reflection. Without introverts, we wouldn't have artists, writers, musicians, scientists, or computer geeks. The extrovert's primary life value is happiness; for introverts, it is meaning. Introverts can even find happiness a distraction from sorting out what has meaning and from being engaged in meaningful activities. Extroverts, of course, find this insane.

Very few people are completely one or the other. Introversion/extroversion exists on a spectrum, with most in the middle. With age, people broaden to incorporate more of the opposite characteristics, becoming less extreme and more moderate. Mature introverts may even enjoy parties and meeting new people, as long as it is balanced with enough time alone. I read once that the least amount of time one can spend at a party without seeming rude is one and a half hours, so I've encouraged my introverted clients to plan to attend social functions for that amount of time only, before escaping home. We all find this a huge relief.

Innies and outies often find each other wrong while it is really a matter of difference. Introverts can feel defective living in the US, and find solace realizing it is purely a cultural prejudice. And for me? Finally, I prefer to go outside and play rather than read a book. As long as that book is waiting when I come back home.

Restaurant Review: Café Wuhu

For starters at this richly poignant little eatery, my charming companion ordered the house signature cocktail, the Robust Symphony, while I enjoyed a gutsy White Zinfandel with resplendent sulfites. We shared the appetizer of Pork Rinds with Pear Grantinee—personally, I found the disodium guanylate to be a touch on the light side, but it was more than compensated for by a flourish of butylated hydroxyanisole.

Our entrees arrived. My Sesame Battered Chicken came bathed in a gravy whose calcium stearoyl lactylate gave it a sleek texture. I usually prefer methyl ethyl cellulose as a thickening agent, but with this dish, my hat's off to the chef. My delightful companion chose the Pizza with Buffalo Wings, Carrot, and Bleu Cheese Dip. I felt it could have been enhanced with decanal dimethyl acetal, although my companion found the sodium aluminum silicate piquant and exciting. We shared a side of the Jalapeño Creamed Corn, a chunky, creamy delight, which was ethereal and riveting and actually edible.

For dessert we split the Bananas Foster on Chocolate Waffle, finding it toothsome and tasty. It was the most delightful Yellow 2G color, exquisitely sweetened with acesulfame potassium and Sucralose. Lesser establishments will substitute neohesperidin dihydrochalcone which often prompts my charming companion to offer me a breath mint.

The complimentary rice pudding brought to mind the great MSG debate with the public outcry that it causes headaches and other ills. All the fuss could have been simply avoided by substituting monoPOTASSIUM glutamate—a flavor enhancer which anyone with a palate will agree is far superior. A potential similar scandal is brewing today regarding polysorbate 65—I agree, the 65 is overkill—the 60 is plenty and the difference, although subtle, is distinct.

We finished our sublime and luscious meal with cappuccinos enhanced by polyethylene glycol 8000—I personally prefer the foam but understand that others may not. The formaldehyde was barely detectable. All and all it was a superb and softly unobtrusive meal, precisely cooked and clearly fragrant. My only wish is that the chef had used more propylparaben so that we could have displayed the leftovers and enjoyed looking at them for years to come.

Preparing for Earthquakes

I've been thinking about the two earthquakes that happened a couple years ago. The one in Haiti got a lot of media coverage; the photos broke our hearts. The deadly, impoverished country was devastated and hasn't recovered to this day.

Many people weren't aware that a quake of far greater magnitude shook Chile, the affluent nation running down the west coast of South America. The Chile quake was 501 times stronger than Haiti's, according to the Huffington Post, and yet we didn't hear much about it because there was very little damage. Chile has had a long history of handling emergencies, so homes and offices were designed to withstand disasters. The country was in all respects better prepared. By contrast, in Haiti there were no building codes, and Haitians had not been schooled in how to react. Although the earthquake was much stronger, the damage was minimal in Chile.

Of course, there is a lesson here that it would behoove all of us to be physically prepared for emergencies. There are easily download-able lists on the Internet of items we should have in our cars and homes for emergencies: bottled water, snacks, blankets, candles, etc., and it's a smart thing to do. It's prudent to be prepared, as Chile was.

But what I've been thinking about is the lesson these earthquakes have to teach us about our emotional lives. People whose lives are stable are like Chile; that is, they are more easily able to deal with an emotional "earthquake" than people whose lives are not.

For example, I often suggest to my single patients that they focus on having enough platonic friends first before they focus on finding a partner. They will be more emotionally prepared for the "earthquakes" of dating if they have enough emotional support in their lives and aren't waiting for their partners to provide that stability.

If you develop emotionally supportive networks around you now, they will be there for you when life brings you an "earthquake," as it inevitably will. Life brings emotional suffering to everyone at some time in their lives. Someone you love will die; someone might leave you; you may have financial difficulties. These events are universally devastating, but if your life is stable, you can survive the earthquake as a prepared country such as Chile did, rather than be rocked to your core and barely able to recover like an impoverished Haiti.

Our Brains Are Starving

The rate of depression increased every year of the last decade after showing a dramatic spike upward in the 1990s. According to the 2011 report from the Centers for Disease Control and Prevention, eleven percent of Americans are taking antidepressant medication, which includes the fact that more than one in five women ages 40-59 are on antidepressants, the highest of any age group.

Why all this unhappiness?

Certainly our brains are overfed with stimuli: visual images, facts and information, celebrity gossip, and the news. Never have people desired as much from life or expected to get it: perfect bodies, perfect health, perfect relationships, wealth and fame. We are constantly being sold superficial values which cannot bring fulfillment, leading to extremes of loneliness and despair.

In addition to the stress of unrealistic expectations, our brains are malnourished from our lousy diets. We've all heard about how badly we eat, our food loaded up on fat, sugar, and chemicals. The depleted soil leaves our food devoid of nutrition. Caffeine, alcohol, and sugar cause blood sugar drops that lead to mood swings, anxiety, and depression. We worry about the effects on our bodies but forget to consider what it does to our brains.

Our diet of processed foods is starving our brains of the neurotransmitters we need to be happy. People "develop emotional symptoms as a direct result of the unavailability of the brain and body chemicals needed for stable feelings, thoughts, and memory," states Joan Matthews Larson, Ph.D., in *Seven Weeks to Sobriety.*

National Institute of Mental Health (NIMH) findings show that the neurotransmitter serotonin is nearly depleted in the brains of people who have committed suicide examined during autopsies.

A whole class of antidepressants has been developed to regulate serotonin. These drugs are effective for many people and have brought much relief.

But stress and poor nutrition can nullify these effects. If you do not take in enough protein, vitamins, or minerals to build the neurotransmitters, an imbalance develops. In addition to improving one's diet, natural supplements have been found helpful. In my opinion, all people suffering from depression should be taking fish oil for Omega-3 fatty acids daily. There is also compelling research on the use of amino acids, Sam-E, St. John's Wort, DHEA, and B vitamins.

The truth is, many unhappy people will not find relief from their symptoms until they control their diets with the stringency of the diabetic, learning to eat fresher and healthier foods and taking supplements. If you're one of the many struggling with problematic moods, it's certainly worth a try.

What Are the Causes of Lifelong Depression?

Some unfortunate people suffer from depression all their lives. There may be a sneaking suspicion it's their fault in some way, which is not true. Lifelong (chronic) depression is an illness that can be as debilitating as heart disease, and if untreated can even be fatal. Chronic depression is caused by one or a combination of the following:

Physical

- You have an imbalance in your brain chemistry. This can be addressed through supplements and/or antidepressant medications. Many people think they don't want to take medication, but what if your prejudice against it is keeping you from relief?

- You don't get enough exercise. Research has repeatedly shown that getting enough exercise is the number one thing that helps relieve depression.

- You are lacking EFA's and need to take fish oil supplements. This seems to be especially true of people of Northern European heritage.

- You have a highly sensitized reaction to alcohol, sugar, and/or caffeine and may not be able to use them like other people. Bummer, I know, but many people with chronic depression see miraculous results when they begin to manage their diets in much the same way a diabetic does.

Psychological

- There are ways that you think and things you tell yourself that are not helpful. Depressed people tend to have depressing thoughts. You do not have to be a slave to your mind.

- You don't have enough friends or social contact. Depressed people tend to be lonely without adequate social support. Facebook doesn't count—we need to be in the presence of other people's bodies.

- You have unfinished business from the past that needs to be worked through. A competent, licensed mental health professional can help you do the work to get free.

Spiritual

- You are not living your right life. Depressed people often feel trapped in work that is not feeding their hearts or their passions. There are hard decisions that must be made if they are to feel good about themselves and their lives.

- You are a spiritual person, and living a life without deeper meaning is not enough for you. Many depressed people have tasted something deeper than is offered by the mainstream culture and have a driving desire to honor that inner knowing. This call must be answered.

The healing of lifelong (chronic) depression takes a holistic approach, and yes, it can be done. If you or someone you love suffers, please get competent help.

It's Hard to Be Creative
When You're Hungry

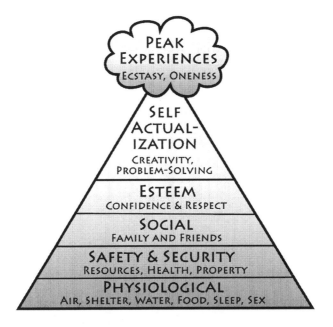

Remember Maslow's Hierarchy of Needs? I think about it a lot when I try to explain to people what Transpersonal Psychology is, or what it is that a transpersonal therapist does that is different from traditional counseling.

Maslow theorized that there is an order in which human needs must be met: for example, if you're lacking food and

41

shelter, it's going to be hard to think about optimizing your creativity. You will need to concentrate on finding food first. Likewise, if you're feeling as if you don't have enough love in your life, it's going to be hard to focus on achievement and what you'd like to give to the world.

The Hierarchy of Needs is shaped like a pyramid, with the bottom rung being Physiological Needs (survival: food, water, sleep, etc.), followed by Safety Needs (security of the body, employment, resources, family, health, comfort). When these needs have been satisfied, we begin to consider Love/ Belonging (friendship, family, sexual intimacy), the need for Esteem (confidence, achievement, respect for and by others). Some people actually develop to the point of reaching Self Actualization (creativity, spontaneity, problem solving), and on the top some add the need for Peak Experiences (ecstasy, sense of Oneness).

As people lucky enough to have been born in the West, very few of us are grappling with Physiological Needs. Most of us don't need to spend our days looking for food like some in Africa or deep in the Amazon jungle. Most of us are lucky enough to have employment, which is a different level of concern than that of the right employment, which is our higher need for Self Actualization. Many people who come to therapy are working on the level of Esteem Needs, especially if they grew up in difficult families where their esteem was not allowed to flourish or was broken by abuse.

When people come in for a therapy consult, one thing the therapist might look at is where their concerns are on the pyramid. Is this a person who has trouble providing basic care for herself? Is he able to feel safe in the world? Is it relationship problems? Or an existential question of what it all means? Each of these concerns would take different efforts for resolution.

The promise of technology was that people would be freed from lower level needs to be able to focus on the higher. However, it seems that in America we have become trapped trying to solve the same needs over and over. It is helpful to think of moving to the higher levels after the lower have been met: self actualization and peak experiences, which is really spiritual search.

44

Chapter 2

We're Still Mammals, You Know

Madison's Apple Tree

Madison is as wide eyed as any child has ever been watching her seedling push its way up out of the Styrofoam cup. Like many kindergarten kids in America, her class has planted apple seeds and is waiting for them to grow. The children tend the plants lined up on the windowsill, learning that they require water, sunlight, and tender loving care. The students are taught about photosynthesis and the making of chlorophyll. Mostly, they learn about patience—that growing things take their own time no matter how much we might like to rush them.

When the experiment is over, Madison takes the cup home, and her dad offers to plant the tiny treasure. Outside the classroom environment, the little tree is fragile and helpless, sitting beside the driveway near a clump of bushes. It could easily be run over by the lawnmower, or dogs, or somebody clumsily getting out of a car. The new-born little shoot needs protection, so Madison's dad puts a wire cage around it, the kind he uses for tomatoes. Once the plant are sturdy, he will remove the support and it will stand on its own.

People who are in intense periods of personal growth often need similar protection. When someone has had success clearing out a major piece of old baggage, or is in shock at encountering unexpected trauma, s/he is raw, and a new way of seeing, of being, is growing in them. This newness is a good thing, but the sprout is vulnerable, untested, and in need of shielding to ensure its continued growth.

Because in this culture we are expected to be always happy and chipper, we lack the understanding that at certain times of life it is okay and even preferable to retreat for a while behind a wall of safety. This might mean staying in instead of going out; only hanging out with gentle, nurturing people instead of people who won't understand; special self-care such as getting massages, eating comfort foods, listening to chill music, or being in silence. We learn to appreciate that personal growth is a process that will take its own time no matter how much we might like to rush it, and that in the beginning it is fragile and needs to be protected against the outside world. Madison's sweet little apple tree needs protection while it is growing, and precious human beings do too.

Myself Only Smaller

"Why didn't I say something? I was so stupid! Why didn't I stop the abuse?" Emily is crying as she recounts a painful memory that affects the way she relates to men in the present.

Often, my patients who are involved in processing painful wounds from childhood have trouble forgiving themselves. They feel they should have known better or handled things differently. It's common in the consultation room as well as out on the street for people to blame themselves because in their early years they were not as smart, educated, assertive, or as neurologically mature as they are today.

When I looked into this, I went back in time and there I was, myself only smaller. In my childhood memories, I am as I am today only my body is tiny. It doesn't make any sense, of course, but everyone I've talked to remembers a smaller version of how they are today, rather than remembering the emotional experience of the time.

But that's not how it was. Back then, like all children, each of us was innocent, completely lacking in worldly wisdom or the street smarts that come from the school of hard knocks. We were utterly dependent on the adults in our environment for everything: food, shelter, for life itself. Our emotions were not mature, and our nervous systems had not yet developed. We weren't able to make adult decisions, reason things out, or protect ourselves from harm. Emily didn't stop the abuse because she hadn't yet matured into the perceptive person she is today who would handle things differently.

Years ago in my own therapy, I was clearing trauma that had happened when I was eleven years old. I was baffled as to why the incident had hurt me so much. Pondering this, I walked over to a playground and looked at an actual eleven-year-old girl. She looked so innocent and fragile that I began to cry. I saw she needed protection and was obviously too little to have understood what was happening to her. It changed forever how I thought about my own experience and the traumatic experiences of others.

I often encourage patients to go look at some kids if they don't have any of their own. It helps tremendously. I'm not trying to create a new breed of voyeurs or playground stalkers—you can also visit children of friends or relatives if you have them. It really helps to see their innocence and to recall your own vulnerability, trust, and sweetness. You were smaller, yes, but not just a smaller version of yourself today.

You Don't Need to Love Yourself First

"You have to love yourself first before you can love anyone else." Justin is saying this as his explanation for why he's still single. It's an adage we've all heard a zillion times, haven't we? I used to blindly believe it myself—I'd heard it over and over and read it in self-help books, so it must be true.

It's considered so absolutely right, it's not even questioned. I hear it frequently quoted by my patients and friends. But think it through with me:

Many people out there in long-term relationships don't particularly love themselves, and didn't love themselves before they got paired up either. They didn't wait until they loved themselves to get involved.

You don't need to be a good tennis player before you decide to learn to play tennis. People at all levels of competency enjoy playing. Some of them don't even particularly love tennis; they just play for the fun of it.

Relationships are petri dishes in which we can learn to love ourselves and others. Through the constant friction, through correcting our mistakes and starting over again, through striving to become a better person, we gradually turn into someone who is capable of love. All that is really needed

51

is a willingness to love and be loved and a decision to not have to get your own way all the time.

People who don't especially love themselves yet, usually because of a difficult childhood or because they are sensitive to advertisers' messages that they don't measure up, can learn to love themselves by being in relationships. As the slogan goes in Alanon, "Let us love you until you learn to love yourself."

We don't learn to love in a vacuum. It's essential to have relationships with other people in order to turn into a person who loves yourself, and not the other way around. The famous saying above is putting the cart before the horse.

You don't need to wait until you learn to love yourself before you start loving others. Go ahead and love freely: rescue a cat or dog, become friendly with everyone, not just people your own age or coolness-factor. Help out; volunteer. Join groups and give, give, give. You learn to love yourself by becoming a lover and not by waiting until you've reached some mythical state.

Learning to Speak French

People who grow up in difficult families miss learning some of life's most basic skills. In homes where physical abuse is present, for example, children often don't grow up with the understanding that their bodies deserve respect. If the parents were emotionally cold, the child misses learning what it's like to live in a world where affection is easy and can be taken for granted. Kids grow into adults who don't believe they can fend for themselves when their parents are controlling and over-protective.

A common thread running through these challenging environments is an inability to speak the language of feelings. These kinds of families often have unspoken rules about not feeling, not speaking about feelings, or not feeling feelings they believe are incorrect to feel. Not learning the language of feelings can lead to alienation from oneself and others.

It's as if your parents didn't teach you how to speak French, and you suddenly realize you're living in a world where everyone speaks French but you. Yes, it's a handicap, but you can learn, even at the advanced age you are now. You will have to work on it diligently, but it can be done.

The first step is learning that feeling feelings is okay and to welcome their presence in your life. Next is to learn the names of the various feeling states and their many gradations. Sometimes I'll give my patients a simple chart with faces mimicking the various emotions such as anger, happiness, or fear, and we'll go through them methodically noticing the attendant physical response. The patient begins a process of checking in with their body to identify what they are feeling. They learn to bypass the mind, that purveyor of false information.

Patients practice "speaking French" during the week between sessions and report back what it is like to identify their feelings and live with their responses. The next stage is to practice expressing these feelings in words, both in the therapy session and with trusted people in the patient's life. Expressing feelings to a loved one can lead to closeness and intimacy, often of a type which the patient has never experienced before.

It is certainly harder to learn French when you're an adult than if you had grown up bilingual at home, but we all know people who have done it. It is quite possible to become fluent in a second language and enjoy eloquently conversing with friends, writing poems and sonnets and essays, and who knows, maybe even sharing a few jokes.

"When in Doubt, Blame Your Parents"

This was a slogan on a card I received that I've never thrown out because it makes me laugh every time I see it. That would be an easy out, right? You don't need to accept responsibility for yourself because your parents made you the way you are. If you do something harmful to yourself or someone else, it's not your fault; it's your parents'!

Sounds silly put that way, but you'd be surprised. People who had difficult childhoods sometimes use that as a justification for why their lives are not working today. Oprah Winfrey, certainly a successful person, has shared that she overcame being sexually molested as a child; obviously, she didn't consider that an excuse. There are many people who had traumatic childhoods whose lives are flourishing, so we really can't blame the parents.

Clients in therapy may be reticent to do historical work because they love their parents, feel loyalty to them, and don't want to blame them. The clients are afraid we're going to find out the parents were villains, which is rarely the case. Usually, although not always, our parents were well-meaning people like ourselves doing the best they could with what was handed down from their own parents.

It's not necessary to stop loving your parents to see what they taught you that wasn't helpful, but it is necessary to identify the messages from the parents that were not accurate. I sometimes call these false messages "brainwashing" to underscore for clients just how strong this conditioning can be.

If, for example, you were taught that sex is sinful, you might want to change that brainwashing. If you were taught that you should never speak up, that your ideas are nonsense, or that you don't have your own special form of attractiveness—these beliefs taught by well-meaning parents are not helpful in the world of adults and would benefit from examination, then elimination.

In psychotherapy, we're not about blaming your parents. We are about you examining the things your parents instilled in you that are not helpful and throwing them out with the trash. But, we want to make sure you do keep the many useful things your parents passed on. We don't want to interfere with you having the best relationship possible with them. The more love in the world, the better.

Politically Correct Emotions

Once when I was a little girl, my father said to me, "Stop crying. You're too smart to have feelings." He was my perfect dad (until adolescence anyway), so it seemed he must be right. He never stopped trying to get everyone in the house, my mother, my brother, my sisters and me, to stop expressing our emotions, although he met with minimal success.

There's a prevailing notion in our culture that you shouldn't have emotions, or if you do, only the "positive" ones. It's okay to be happy, cheerful, and outgoing, but even if you're happy, be careful not to be too exuberant. We wouldn't want people dancing in the streets!

Then there's the New Age tyranny that only certain emotions are politically correct. To be a superior person, you're supposed to go around with a feeling of gratitude at all times. Anger, grief, disgust, resentment, pain, hopelessness—these are signs that you are not who you ought to be, and certainly, "not spiritual."

In fact, however, all emotions are an essential aspect of what it means to be alive. Your grief is beautiful, your shyness, your reticence, your pain and hopelessness. All of these emotions are the truth of your life and everyone's life, so why would you want to miss knowing this? Every single human being has been hit with crippling grief—no one gets out without having their heart broken. If you don't experience the richness of your grief, the way it deepens you and opens your heart, you will not share this universal experience. What gets lost in these rules-not-to-feel is what it means to be human.

If you observe, you will notice that your feelings come and go like the weather. Some days it rains; some days the sun shines, but none of it lasts. We all know the weather will change and expect it to. Feelings are the same—if you watch them and allow them to be as they are, you will notice them morphing and changing—floating by like clouds.

Instead of standing guard over yourself to make sure you only experience the correct emotions, how delightful instead to watch the passing parade of human feelings that float through like the weather, ever changing. If you remain at war with your emotional life, you run the risk of missing the truth of yourself, the truth of the experience of your life.

The Cats Were Still Suckling

On my 16th birthday, I asked for a cat of my own: a delicate and high-strung silver point Siamese. I named her Ina after a cat that lived on the shoulder of a hippie I'd met downtown the previous summer. Ina was a very anxious cat, not in small part because of the way we taunted and teased her.

Ina produced a litter of kittens whose father we never identified because the kittens were pure black. It was a pretty, interracial sight to watch her lying there, the white and silver mom with her pure black brood lined up nursing on her.

But something went wrong as the cats grew because they never weaned. When they were bigger than she was, they would be lined up, still suckling. We would shoo and, I'm sorry to say, slap them away to no avail. We'd come back later, and they'd be feasting again.

I have a patient whose 25-year old son has moved back home and she is supporting him, both of them blaming the economy. I understand that finding a job can be challenging, especially for many young people just out of college. But this mother is interfering with her son growing up and emancipating. He's "still suckling" when he's bigger than she is.

In humans, it's called "codependence" when we do for

59

another adult something they should be doing themselves. It doesn't help them; instead, it infantilizes and keeps them child-like and dependent. For each person in a codependent relationship, growth is stunted. Each needs to let go, wean, and get on with their life.

In addition to the son in the above relationship needing to move on and create his own adult life, the mother needs to let go of being an actively involved mother and deal with her sadness about her empty nest. Only then will she be able to create a fulfilling post-mothering life for her later years.

For humans who are struggling with codependency, we are lucky to have 12-step groups like Alanon and Codependents Anonymous and the classic self-help book *Codependent No More* by Melody Beattie. For cats like Ina and her babies, maybe someone will eventually step up to the plate and start self-help groups for other species. Any takers?

You Don't Have to Kill Your Parents

Philip Larkin, one of the stellar poets of the twentieth century, famously wrote:

Your mum and dad, they fuck you up,
They may not mean to, but they do.
They fill you with the fears they had,
And add some extra just for you.

Everyone could benefit from identifying where their parents "f*cked" them up and working through it. In fact, being clear of non-useful parental programming is an essential milestone on the psychological and spiritual path. If you're stuck with pain, upset, or wishing anything were different about your childhood, you can't progress to a space of having more interesting problems to solve.

In one of the Castaneda books, Don Juan instructed his apprentice, Carlos, "You have to kill your parents." People are willing to move across the country, if not the world, to create distance between themselves and their parents and "kill" their presence in their lives, but it's really internal distance they are seeking: separation from expectations, a separate identity, and freedom from parental do's and don'ts.

Helping people get unstuck from their parents is one of

61

the things we do in psychotherapy. In some cases, it can be completed relatively quickly; in others, it takes lengthy excavation work, depending on the severity of the trauma suffered, and how deeply it is lodged in the cells and tissues of the body. It's more complicated, of course, if there's been abuse, but everyone must separate themselves from the parts of the parents' message that is not them. When the work is successful, a new person emerges who is uniquely one's self, taking the best that the parents gave them, and released from what doesn't fit. It can be hard work, but freedom is worth every iota of effort and commitment.

It's possible to come to a place where there's no pain left, no more anger or resentment, no heat, no charge. Once you "kill" your parents and your unhealthy attachment to them, you become free to love them for the first time, to meet them as one adult to another rather than as a child to parent. To progress along life's path, you must come to a place where you're not afraid of anything that's inside any more. And that is possible for you.

Leonard Orr, the inventor of Rebirthing, said, "If you don't hate your parents, you haven't even started." Is it time for you to complete this stage of your development once and for all?

What Difference Does it Make Whether You Like it or Not?

Most mornings, I go to the gym. I say "hi" to Casey at the front desk and several of the other regulars who work out at the same time. We complete our routines with as little thought as possible, doing what needs to be done in order to stay in shape, and hopefully getting strong and toned in the process.

On most days, you'll see a newbie being taken through the beginners' circuit by one of the trainers. Last week, it was an overweight middle-aged woman who was stretching and groaning, dressed in a yellow-flowered t-shirt rather than the sleek colorless wear the serious athletes affect. She had obviously not been to the gym enough to have started enjoying it.

Her trainer was having her do reps on the Inner Thigh Extender. "I don't like this one," she said, pouting.

I laughed out loud and smiled with her and Trevor, the trainer. "What difference does that make?" I asked. We shared a chuckle, commiserating. Those of us who are already in shape lost interest long ago in whether we like an exercise or not. We just do it because it needs to be done.

The same is true of food. People who are slim and healthy don't focus much on whether or not they like the foods they are eating; instead, they eat foods that will keep them that way. They'll dine on egg whites and chicken breasts and more vegetables daily than most people eat in a week. And it's not because they particularly like it—they like the results.

Some of my patients have trouble because they won't do what they don't want to do. With them, I share one of my definitions of adulthood: adults are people who are willing to do what they don't want to do. They've accepted that life requires the performance of seemingly endless irksome tasks: housework, paperwork, paying taxes, picking up socks off the floor where we left them. Life works better when we get over our childish belief that life should unfold according to our preferences.

Some people have been spoiled by phrases such as "Follow Your Bliss" taken out of context to mean that you should only do what gives you pleasure. If you're a person whose life is not working, it might help to stop paying so much attention to your personal likes and dislikes and get on with what needs to be done. You'll like the results.

You Have to Let Them Drown

You're enjoying the perfect stroll along the beach: the crunch of sand between your toes, the lapping waves, the glorious sun on your face. You notice the wind caressing your hair—suddenly you hear cries for help!—the agony of a fellow being beginning to drown. Your impulse is to heroically swim out, drag the person to shore, provide mouth-to-mouth resuscitation and thereby save a life.

Have you heard about this? That's the exact thing you must not do. Unless you're a trained lifeguard and know how to help, you can't go in the water. A drowning person, in their panic, will pull you under in an attempt to save themselves, and there will be two drowned persons instead of one. It's a nasty fact, but if you want to save a life, the only thing you can do is summon help.

Even if it's a family member, you can't go in unless you've received training in saving lives. Standing on the shore, knowing you can't help: heartbreaking. Choosing to save your own life rather than two people dying: excruciatingly painful.

"Dan" is a patient of mine who has reached a certain degree of success with his acting. He has all the talent, looks, and charisma needed, but lacks the persistence to complete the daily tasks to further his career. In therapy, we've been examining his close bond with his family back in the Midwest who are uniformly depressed, unhappy with their lives, and lack the will to change. There are unwritten rules that family members are not supposed to become too successful, or stray too far from unhappiness. In other words, Dan's family is drowning, and in an effort to try and save them, Dan is being sucked down and is drowning along with them.

Dan and I have been talking about how he needs to "let his parents drown." He's not trained in lifesaving. If he wants, he can go back to school, study psychotherapy or social work, and change his profession to become a "trained lifeguard." But even those of us who are, aren't effective working with our own families.

Although it is painful to stand on the shore and realize that someone you love is drowning and you cannot save them, it is a decision you must make in order that your own life be saved. Certainly you can try to summon help by pointing them to therapy, but they may not choose to go. It's essential that at least one life be saved. It's time for you to become free and save yourself.

Premature Forgiveness

Many people who come to see me announce that they have already forgiven the people who hurt them, so the work is done. They've read in spiritual books that forgiveness is the key, so wanting to be good people, they are anxious to forgive and forget. Unfortunately, it's not that simple.

This type of forgiveness is done from the level of the mind, by making a decision to think about the situation differently, which is as helpful as putting a Band-Aid on a broken arm. The pain happened emotionally, physically, and/or sexually, and must be dealt with on these levels. For the mind to pronounce that "all is forgiven" is New Age nonsense, as if all it takes to come to forgiveness is to pronounce it so.

To truly get to a state of forgiveness, you must first fully experience the feelings associated with the betrayal or abuse. This doesn't mean that you need to act the feelings out, become overly dramatic, or hang onto them for years. But it does mean that the energetic frequency of the emotion needs to be allowed to pass through the physical body on its way out. When forgiveness is merely an idea or a mental construct pasted over the inner rage, horror, betrayal, hurt, or anger, the emotions will continue to exert pressure to be released. When through the process of therapy we drain those feelings, leaving the person free and cleansed, the forgiveness process can begin.

It's understandable that a person would want to bypass this step, because dealing with these historical emotions can be intense. The work is hard, but it is worth doing. To be free of blame and resentment is worth the pain it takes to clear it out of your system. It can be done. Get some help so that it's not just a mental exercise.

If you try to forgive prematurely, or before you have done your work, you run the risk of being stuck with painful feelings lying hidden underneath everything you do. When you explore and confront past emotional wounds, eventually you will come to accept the humanity of whoever harmed you, along with the realization that we all hurt each other. Then true forgiveness is possible and when it comes from that genuine place, it will flow out like the love that it truly is.

So What if You're a Little Off?

We were talking about Ezra Pound in my writing group the other week—about how he revolutionized poetry and writing in general by his idea that it's all about the image rather than storytelling. I'd read that he'd spent thirteen years in a mental hospital so I said, "Of course, he could see things differently— he was mentally ill."

The others in the group recoiled. They thought I was making a value judgment and being mean, but I'm around mental illness all day when I'm working as a therapist, so it doesn't seem like a bad thing to me. Also, for twelve years I worked in mental hospitals so I don't have any beef with mental illness. Sometimes, it's not wrong at all.

Here's a shortlist of people who suffered from severe mental illness and still made significant contributions to humanity:

> Sylvia Plath
> Beethoven
> Kurt Cobain
> F. Scott Fitzgerald and his wife, Zelda
> Ernest Hemingway
> Vincent Van Gogh
> Virginia Woolf

These folks gave great gifts to the world with their significantly different ways of perceiving. They were able to step outside the mainstream long enough to nurture their own uniqueness.

In this culture, we are sold an image of what constitutes sanity that is extremely superficial and soul-less. The healthy person is supposed to be robotically "happy" all the time, constantly productive and striving toward material success—outwardly focused, extroverted, socially slick, and looking the way we're all aware we're supposed to look. If your nature is different from this, something is wrong with you that needs to be fixed.

People who are, say, sensitive, isolative, and introspective, are often are led to believe they are defective in some way. I meet people all the time who think there is something wrong with them when the only thing wrong is not accepting their own humanity.

I'm not suggesting that having a mental illness isn't a painful way to live, nor am I of the school that romanticizes it, like the filmmakers of the 60s who tried to convince us that the people inside the asylum were sane, and those outside were crazy—that's just not true. There are states of consciousness that do not allow one to adequately care for oneself, have loving relationships, or enjoy one's life, and if that is the case, psychotherapy can help.

Why stigmatize people who have mental illness as any worse than people with physical illness? I say embrace the unique emanation that is you, and reject the constant pressure to be like Tony Robbins or Cameron Diaz. Plenty of people have already got that down. Maybe we need another introspective soulful poet or a wildly flamboyant fiction writer. We need people with out-of-the-mainstream views. If the pain of the way you are is too much, get help. But we surely wouldn't want to make you sane.

Chapter 3

Technologies For Change

Sunshine in a Box

As the days grow darker in the fall and winter, so do many peoples' moods. 10% or more of the population in northern climates may suffer from Seasonal Affective Disorder (SAD), a type of depression that is cyclical and affected by the time of year. Symptoms include feelings of hopelessness, low self-esteem, poor concentration, low energy or fatigue, and problems with eating and/or sleeping.

SAD is most often treated the same way depression is: with medication. However, SAD sufferers looking for holistic options are in luck. Since research suggests that SAD is caused by the diminished light during the winter months, effective treatment has been developed using electrical light boxes that mimic the sun's rays. "Light therapy is a way to treat seasonal affective disorder (SAD) by exposure to artificial light. It is safe and has few side effects," states the Mayo Clinic (2010). A Canadian study (*American Journal of Psychiatry*, 2006) found light therapy and fluoxetine, better known as Prozac, to be equally effective.

I decided to use myself as a guinea pig so I ordered a light box online. The process was easy, with prices ranging from $120-150. When the light box arrived, I started my treatment, about 15 minutes a day of exposure. The light is supposed to shine indirectly into your eyes rather than directly, so I put the box, about the size of a coffee table book, on the side of my desk. It beamed the measured dose of light while I drank my morning coffee and perused Facebook. I noticed a positive effect on my mood right away. In fact, it felt so good I gave myself three more doses, an overdose which produced a headache.

Light box therapy should be done in the morning, as it may be too stimulating later in the day. It's important to keep a consistent schedule during the winter months. If you stop too soon when you think you're improving, you'll miss the cumulative effect which helps bring positive results. Some people experience immediate relief as I did; for others, it may take a week of treatments or longer.

Light therapy is often not enough on its own to provide a cure for SAD. The treatment of any type of depression demands a well-rounded approach. Exercise, psychotherapy, meditation, increasing pleasurable activities, being around other people and not isolating yourself, and even medication: all these are important components of a holistic treatment plan. But if you've noticed a correlation between bad weather and bad moods, light box therapy can be a valuable tool for recovery. It's certainly made a difference for me.

The Self Esteem Issue

Many people conceptualize that their problem is "low self esteem." Their belief is that when they start feeling better about themselves, they will act to improve their lives. Often the student therapists I teach agree and want to design therapy to address this. To me, they have all got it backwards.

Back in the 90s, schools across the US started programs to boost self esteem. They were influenced by California's Task Force to Promote Self-Esteem and Personal and Social Responsibility. Children were taught self-affirmative jingles and songs. Contests were held in which everyone received a trophy although no one actually won. Methods were invented by well-meaning people who believed that by encouraging self esteem, they were giving kids a better chance at success.

Nowadays, the school self esteem movement is widely considered to have been an enormous failure. On an international test, American kids were at the top of the charts in believing they are good in math, yet they ranked low on math skills. A generation or two of students were evaluated as entitled and under-performing. Research published in 2004 found that, against expectation, higher self-esteem was not correlated with better learning or behavior.

We need to look a little deeper into this question of self esteem. Self esteem needs to be earned by living in a way that is estimable, or, as the 12-Step slogan goes, by performing estimable acts. If someone's actions are not worthy of esteem, it is good that they feel unhappy with themselves and their actions. As an example, we could agree that a criminal ripping off the monthly checks of the elderly does not deserve high self esteem, no matter how many jingles he repeats.

Most of us have an internal compass that tells us whether we are living right or not. When we are not, our self esteem goes down as an indicator that we are off track. If, instead of paying attention to this we attempt to overlook it by self esteem exercises or reciting affirmations, we miss the opportunity to grow. Instead, we ought to take a painful look at how we need to change to be worthy of high self regard.

If we are contributing through our work, if we share loving relationships, if we are not holding ourselves out to be better than others, if we act as stewards for planet earth; we are worthy of good self esteem, and we will feel it. Children can be taught that they can earn self worth rather than merely expect it. For it is our actions that matter in the long run, not our beliefs about ourselves.

Top Ten Non-Drug Treatments for Depression

Many of my patients do not want to take medication, and I support their efforts to find a holistic solution. Here are my top recommendations:

1) **Exercise:** Believe it or not, exercise has been found to be the most effective treatment for depression. Of course, that's the last thing you feel like doing when you're feeling down. The minimum requirement is 3 times per week for 20 minutes. More is better.

2) **Weekly Psychotherapy:** Long standing issues, family and cultural programming, habits of mind—these are just some of the issues that might be at cause. Depression is a sign that something in your life is not right. Get some help to deal with it.

3) **Check your pleasures:** Coffee, alcohol, sugar, and recreational drugs can lead to mood disorders. Even moderate use can be too much for depressed persons. Observe how your moods go up and down with use.

4) **Supplements:** All people suffering from depression should be taking fish oil for Omega-3 Fatty Acids daily.

There is also compelling research on the use of Amino Acids, Sam-E, St. John's Wort, DHEA, and B vitamins. Read up and experiment.

5) **Sunlight:** It helps to get direct sun exposure every day if possible. If not available, a light box can bring a lot of relief. You can easily get your dose of light by sitting in front of one for 15 minutes a day. Light boxes are great.

6) **Regular human contact:** Many people are depressed because they are too isolated. We are social animals. Go to *Meetup.com* and find some people who enjoy the same things as you do.

7) **Challenge your thinking:** Depressed people have depressed thoughts. A book that can be really helpful with this is *Feeling Good* by Dr. David Burns.

8) **Good nutrition:** The way we eat may have a lot to do with fostering depression. Check out *The Mood Cure* by Julia Ross, *Potatoes Not Prozac* by Kathleen DesMaisons, and *Seven Weeks to Sobriety* by Joan Matthews Larson.

9) **Yoga and Meditation:** These are recommended for mild to moderate depression only. Severely depressed people need to become more active and outer focused.

10) **Are you living your right life?** Sometimes depression is an indication that things need changing. Sometimes drastically. Do an inventory of your life.

If these treatments have been tried and there is no change in a month, it is recommended that you get a full evaluation by a healthcare professional. It is important to rule out a medical condition such as low thyroid which would cause depressive symptoms.

Many people consider taking antidepressants a sign of weakness. It is not, any more than is weak for a diabetic to take insulin. Depression is one of the most debilitating illnesses, with many people dying from it each year. It does not make you a better person to endure needless suffering.

Top Ten Non-Drug Treatments for Anxiety

Many of my patients do not want to take medication for anxiety, and I support their efforts to find a holistic solution. Here are my top recommendations:

1) **Practice some deep, slow breaths**: all the way down, pushing your abdomen out. There's a reason the Buddha is always pictured as having a big belly—belly breathing produces calm, chill people. Yoga and meditation classes can help you learn about this.

2) **Be in the Present:** Anxiety is worrying about the future. If you are in the present moment, the now, it is actually impossible to feel anxious.

3) **Take a walk:** In addition to being good for your body and causing a change of scene, walking balances the two sides of the brain.

4) **Download relaxation CDs and/or music:** something that you know is guaranteed to calm you. Make a playlist you can count on to always put you in a relaxed mood.

5) **Watch a comedy:** a movie, some stand-up or even read a comic writer. Laughter may or may not be the best medicine, but it will certainly take your mind off your

troubles.

6) **Get a massage:** Where I live in LA, there are many opportunities to get a low-cost massage, including the new Chinese Foot Massage places that offer an hour-long full-body treatment for $25. Some towns have low-cost massage schools which accept clients.

7) **The calming effect of warmth:** Take a hot bath, drink some hot tea, wrap yourself in a "blankie" and cuddle up on the couch.

8) **Challenge your thinking:** Anxious people have a particular way of talking to themselves that contributes to anxiety. A book that can be really helpful with this is *Feeling Good* by Dr. David Burns.

9) **Good nutrition:** The way we eat may have a lot to do with fostering anxiety. Too much coffee, refined carbohydrates, additives, and sugar can lead to anxiety disorders. Observe how your moods go up and down with use.

10) **Weekly psychotherapy:** Long standing issues, family and cultural programming, habits of mind—these are just some of the issues that might be at cause. Anxiety is a sign that something in your life is not right. Get help to deal with it.

If these treatments have been tried and there is no change in a month, it is recommended get a full evaluation by a healthcare provider. It is important to rule out a medical condition which might cause symptoms of anxiety.

How to Tell if Therapy Is Working

Months went by while I considered leaving therapy. It didn't feel as if we were getting anywhere. At times my therapist, of whom I was very fond, would say something insightful and I'd decide to stay. Then it'd be back to the same dilemma session after session, we're not getting anywhere—should I leave?

The answer is yes. Here's an example of therapy that's working:

"After having finished therapy, I am more comfortable with a larger range of emotions," my friend Jaret recently posted on Facebook, "and as a result, my new music is so organic and emotional." With the help of his therapist, "I was able to watch the traumas change to a more objective point of view and their impact diminished to the point of a lesson learned, kind of like a sign on a road pointing the direction to the next exit."

Therapy is working if the results can be measured in your life as Jaret's can. You've become creatively unstuck, or you're better at your job, less anxious, feel better about life and are not in despair any more. Maybe you're more able to make a decent living, or your relationships have improved, and you feel less lonely. You notice you have increased compassion for yourself and your fellow human beings.

The therapy that I didn't find helpful meandered all over the place with no seeming goal other than increased understanding and the ability to speak in psychological jargon. Some therapists work to foster insight which is fine if it leads to improved action in the world. If your life's not working, insight without changed behavior can actually be harmful, cultivating a retreat from life and an attitude of superiority. Some therapists view their job as acting as a cheerleader, which is okay if that's what you're looking for, but it would be preferable to learn how to find support in the real world rather than paying someone to be your friend.

You and your therapist need to be able to articulate where you are, where you're going, and how much progress you've made in the time you've been working together. If this isn't happening, you're wasting your time and money.

Jack Canfield, although he recommends psychotherapy, states in his book *The Success Principles* that only 20% of therapists are any good. If, like me, you've been wondering whether or not your therapy is working, bring up your concerns with your therapist, and see what she says. It might be time to make a switch.

What to Do Between Sessions

People who are new to psychotherapy often wonder what they should be doing in the time between sessions. Anxious to grow and evolve, they're unsure how to aid the process, and their appointment next week seems far in the future.

The psychotherapy sessions themselves are concentrated, intense 50-minute "hours" one or more times a week. They can be a time when you dive into your depths and share things you've never shared before. You might find your sessions head scratching, heart opening, spirit stirring, or all three. They are meant to be a catalyst for your life to improve in a way that is meaningful to you: a seed, so to speak, that sprouts during the week.

So what can you do between sessions to continue, deepen, forward your growth?

- Take some time to think over what we discussed. See what occurs to you, mull it over, meditate on it. Consider, feel, and intuit what may be revealing itself to you.

- Your session may have pointed out ways that you act mechanically in unhelpful patterns learned in childhood. See if you can catch yourself acting unconsciously in any of the ways we discussed. Be gentle with yourself when you do. The awareness of acting in patterned ways not of your creation or consent is revolutionary, even if you never do anything to change them.

- Or, see yourself acting out of your patterns and change them. Observe how you would previously act in a way not necessarily in your best interest and then act differently in a way that would. Practice this more than once.

- Read books or consult the Internet about your issues. There is a lot of good information out there, and the left brain can be of great assistance. It's usually not enough in itself, but it helps if you are a reading type.

- Write in a journal. Document your growth process, copy down poignant quotes and images that come to you, memories, synchronicities, connections, hunches and humor. If you're not a writer, use another medium: draw, paint, make music, dance.

- Talk to your family or people you grew up with to do some "archaeological research." Call them up or email, and ask questions. It's often useful to find out facts or impressions that were the same or different than yours.

- Do nothing. Go about your life. Open to the awareness that growth is happening. Being quiet and doing nothing, the seed of the session is germinating within you, all by itself.

After The Insight, Now What?

Back in the days when Freudian lying-on-the-couch therapy was all there was, insight into one's problem was considered enough to provide a cure. However, insight-as-cure didn't turn out to be the case—we've all heard about Woody Allen in treatment for decades, his neurosis only growing. Many people walk around with great insight into why they do what they do, baffled as to how to use the information to change their lives.

Caitlin understands there's a correlation between her father's abusiveness and her attraction to unkind men, but still she continues to date them. Josh knows the reason he drinks too much is because he's shy and lonely, but that doesn't help him cut down or stop. Both Caitlin and Josh berate themselves constantly as "stupid" because they know they're smart and have good insight, but neither knows what to do about it.

Do you remember Heisenberg's Uncertainty Principle? The amazing discovery last century that states that just to observe something changes it. To those seeking personal growth, this means that merely the act of observing ourselves will bring about change. However, most of us need to learn to observe ourselves in an entirely different way than we are accustomed: without judgment, not berating ourselves as "stupid," but instead, with awareness and compassion. We develop compassion for ourselves when we accept that we, like everyone else, are caught in not-useful patterns. We can practice calmly observing the impulse to act in ways we don't desire, trapped in patterns we have discovered through our insight.

As we observe and become aware, the next step is to gradually make a series of different decisions. One by one, step by step, different decisions will be made, and behavior will change. After observing her patterns, Caitlin met a man she was really hot for, but after seeing him treat a food server rudely, decided to say "no" to further dates. Josh still has the desire to drink, but one day at a time, he doesn't pick up the glass. Each of these meticulously changed actions is a victory in itself. Slowly but surely, as you too observe yourself with compassion and follow up with different decisions, you will become a new person, more in alignment with your true self.

After the Insight, Part Two

After an important insight into why you act the way you do, the long process of changing your behavior begins, one action at a time. Most people find it difficult to change without outside support, and if that is you, it doesn't mean you're weak or wrong in some way, merely a member of the human race. Here are ten suggestions for finding support:

1. **Keep a journal:** Writing down your thoughts and feelings while observing your growth can be enormously helpful. It's also encouraging to review your progress.

2. **Join a support group:** There are many types of groups, as many as there are problems to solve. Depending on the issues you are working on, this might be Weight Watchers, a walking or work-out team, or a group for adult survivors of sexual abuse.

3. **Find a 12-step group:** Modeled on the successful program of Alcoholics Anonymous, 12-step groups exist for nearly every issue now. The price is right (donation only) and the meetings are filled with "angels" eager to help you for free.

91

4. **Create a supportive environment:** Look around your home to see what changes are needed. For example, you might need to clean the junk food out of your house. Also, this might mean you need new friends or to see less of old ones.

5. **Set measurable goals:** It is hard to know when you reach your goals if they are too broad. "I want to be happy" means something different to each person with that desire. If "happiness" includes losing ten pounds plus having three months savings in the bank, those are measurable steps on the way to happiness.

6. **Reward yourself:** It's important that you celebrate your "wins," the milestones of progress along the way. Maybe you'll buy yourself fresh flowers or go for a massage. Reward yourself frequently for each small gain.

7. **Educate yourself:** Read books and study the Internet to learn what successful people before you have done to change and how they did it.

8. **Find role models:** Sometimes people find it difficult to change because they don't think a clean lifestyle is sexy. Search out people you respect who have what you want and are doing it in a way you admire.

9. **Meditate:** You might like to take time each day to do nothing but sit and be with what is, or it might be useful to spend time focusing on the changes you are trying to make and being grateful for the opportunity to change.

10. **Above all, continue with the psychotherapy** that has helped you. Midway is not the time to stop. After you're firmly rooted in your new life, you'll be ready to fly on your own.

Shortcuts to Mindfulness

The Sleep Stalker

I've been trying to sleep for eight years. Oh, I sleep all right, but I'll wake up at 4 a.m. raring to go with no question of going back to bed. Or I'll stay up late even though I'm exhausted. For a while, I enjoyed it—there's a high that comes from extended periods of no sleep, but every high is followed by its evil twin the low, right? Before this, I used to sleep perfectly every night, no matter what. Here's what I found when I went in search of a cure:

1) **Herbs and Supplements**: Herbal formulas like Calms Forte, soothing teas before bed, melatonin, GABA, inositol, Vitamin B6—although none of these herbal/supplements treatments worked for me, maybe they'll work for you.

2) **Drugs**: Ambien worked for a time. This is the perfect drug, I thought: It does what it says it will do with no hangover. But then the horror set in—'rebound insomnia'—when it suddenly stops working and, in fact, makes your condition worse. Sonata didn't make a dent; Trazadone keeps you asleep for only 4 hours because of its half-life; and Ativan puts you to sleep but leaves horrible enervation and depression the next day. Hardly worth it.

95

3) **Hypnosis**: The sleep CD, *Just Relax – Relaxing to Sleep* by Gail Seymour, worked great for quite awhile—it knocked me out every time. But when it got so I could repeat every word, it wasn't authoritative any more. I tried others but they all had a funny accent or an irritating voice. This is a good place to start if you've never tried them.

4) **Pleasures**: Bad news in this department—both coffee and alcohol seem to be big problems, even if early in the day. I'm still trying to figure out how to make this work short of quitting altogether. Eating before bed only works if it's heavy carbs. The new thinking is that the old standby warm milk actually makes sleeplessness worse because of the protein.

5) **Computer insomnia**: This is actually a new diagnosis. People get so amped up being on the computer late at night that it affects their sleep. Guilty.

6) **Scheduling**: It seems to make a big difference to go to bed and get up at the same time. I've talked to people who had to start putting their sleep first, above anything else, even going out to hear music. Hmmm.

7) **Exercise**: Seems to help with everything. Sometimes, the body is not tired enough to go to sleep.

8) **Creating a sleep palace:** Many times, we need to redo the bedroom—get light blocking curtains, white noise machines, a better mattress. Make the physical space an "invitation for sleep."

9) **Hyperarousal**: Mentally active people tend to exist in this state all the time and are consequently more prone

to insomnia. One has to start consciously relaxing hours before bedtime. A lifestyle makeover is often required.

10) Finally, I read Dr. Barry Krakow who said that if you have insomnia, it's because **you don't want to sleep**. (*Sound Sleep, Sound Mind*, Hoboken, NJ: John Wiley & Sons, 2007) You haven't told yourself that the day is over, and it's time to go to sleep.

I realized this was true. I don't want to sleep—life is just too exciting. I enjoy thinking about things, running the good parts over and over in my mind. At times the bad ones too, although that's another story. Who has time to sleep? It's a shame it's so essential to good heath. If you find the magic key, please let me know.

The Scent of Happiness

Relaxing with friends, chilling to an ambient groove, enjoying the sweet pungent odor of...incense? For most of us, this scene conjures up images of hippies in the 60s: bell bottoms, tie-dye, and never-ending Grateful Dead shows. Actually, it may point to one of the grooviest trends of our time, because according to a recent study, incense can be a potent addition to our strategies for preventive mental health.

Researchers from Johns Hopkins and the Hebrew Universities, in a 2008 study conducted by the Federation of American Societies for Experimental Biology, found that burning incense activates channels in the brain that alleviate anxiety or depression. "In spite of information stemming from ancient texts... most present day worshipers assume that incense burning has only a symbolic meaning," said Raphael Mechoulam, one of the authors of the study. "We found that incense lowers anxiety and causes anti-depressant behavior."

While many people are advocates of aromatherapy, there has been little scientific research conducted to date. "Despite aromatherapy's popularity, efficacy data are scant, and potential mechanisms are controversial," stated the National Center for Complementary and Alternative Medicine (NCCAM) in 2010.

99

One of the few clinical trials that has been conducted was at Ohio State University (2008), which found "robust evidence that lemon oil reliably enhances positive mood regardless of expectancies or previous use of aromatherapy." A prior study published in 1995 in Lancet found that "following a long history in folklore, lavender has been used as a sleep aid, and one small study suggested that it can significantly enhance the amount of time asleep." These results were repeated: "Lavender increased patterns consistent with drowsiness, and subjects reported greater relaxation." (*International Journal of Neuroscience*, 1998)

Even without research, it's common knowledge that things that smell good make us feel good. Laundry right out of the dryer, hot cinnamon rolls, and the smell of a baby's skin are commonly appreciated delights. The aroma of freshly ground coffee is the only thing that entices many of us to get up in the morning. These daily pleasures increase the enjoyment of our lives through their fragrance, so it makes sense that taking the time to literally "smell the roses" leads to a better quality of life.

It will be exciting to watch as more research is conducted verifying the healing properties of scent. In the meantime, it looks as if the hippies might have been on to something. Please pass the patchouli oil.

Staying Sane During the Holidays

The thing that makes the holidays the most difficult is the widespread idea that they shouldn't be. We've been seduced for years by pictures of smiling families passing the turkey and opening their flawlessly wrapped presents. Everyone is easy to get along with, and everyone is perfectly happy.

Nothing could be further from the truth for most people. We are far more complicated creatures than that. All families have their areas of dysfunction which are less likely to politely stay out of sight when everybody is together in the same room.

Liz talked about how she suddenly felt herself becoming a teenager again the minute she walked in the door of her parents' house. "Here I am, a successful person at my job, walking in and going right for the refrigerator and yelling about old unresolved arguments! I hardly recognize myself," she said. When there are injustices that have not been made right, or memories of abuses and unkindness, these things may erupt without warning. "I find myself saying things I later regret," Liz continued. "I always have the best intention to have a wonderful holiday, but it never works out that way." Lowering or "right-sizing" our expectations about the holidays is the first thing that can help.

It's not only family tensions that make the holidays potentially so difficult. Nick talks about how lonely he feels this first season after his divorce: "I guess it's the contrast between then and now, and how disappointed I am about the reality of my life alone. I never thought it'd be this way." This increased isolation and loneliness can also be felt by remembering people who've died.

Stress around finances increases during the holidays. Karen is finding herself limited at what she can actually do. The best thing is for her to make a spending plan of all holiday expenses beforehand and keep to it.

Many of us increase our alcohol intake during the holidays in an attempt to deal with the stress of difficult people and relationships. It's not necessary to stop drinking if this is one of your pleasures, but it helps to be aware of how emotionally destabilized and uncentered too much can leave you. Know your limits or get help to cut down.

Pace yourself during the season, in all areas. Stop trying to be Superwoman. Plan time to be alone and give yourself a break. Delegate what tasks you can. Most of all, tell the truth about how you feel—if you don't feel festive, that's okay. Find at least one person you can talk frankly to who doesn't expect you to act like a perky cheerleader.

If you feel like Scrooge, find somebody safe and tell them about it. Then go back to the party and enjoy the time for what it is—a normal, imperfect holiday season.

Chapter 4

Mastery Of The Normal

But I Don't Want to be Normal!

Justin is a creative person struggling with the evidence that his life is not working. He has no regular source of income, no girlfriend, and nothing to show for his years in LA. He has so many talents he can't figure out his direction, so he keeps starting over, creating plenty of drama. When I suggest that he may need to get a regular job to stabilize his life, his response is, "But I don't want to be normal!"

Believe me, I understand. Back when I was a hippie/beatnik/punk alcohol-abusing waitress in the 70s, dreaming that some day I would be a writer, I despised the word "normal" and all I thought it stood for. "Normal" connoted people who had sold out, people who were not living on the edge, people walking around half asleep, and worst of all, people who had given up on their dreams.

After being lost for longer than I care to mention, one day in a meeting I heard someone say, "I finally believed I was good enough to lead a normal life." I realized that was true about me, too. My desire to not get stuck in a bourgeois life had been motivated partly by my artistic drive, partly by not having high enough regard for myself, and partly by a misunderstanding of how life works.

105

I was lucky enough to find a mentor who taught me that it's a required step to become "normal" in order to get anywhere in life. Unless you are willing to do what it takes to stabilize your finances, living situation, and emotional life, you can't get on to solving more interesting problems. Without this stability, you don't progress, and you keep wondering why your life never amounts to anything. They don't need to be magazine quality, but you'll need a stable home, stable finances, and a stable emotional life to move to the next level.

My mentor, Bill, also taught me that you have to become willing to be bored; otherwise, you'll spend your life chasing drama. You'll make poor decisions such as going back to school instead of buckling down to work, or you'll throw out your perfectly good spouse to buy a more exciting model. You won't mature, because there is always a new drama to solve. As soon as life starts finally coming together and boredom sets in, you'll make a decision to ruin it, chasing what seems more intriguing and less "normal."

To progress beyond sub-normal, Justin will need to pass through "normal" if he ever wants to spend his life in the way he aspires. Normal is a required stage on the way to excellence. What he's seeking is there waiting for him; he just needs to do the work. He hasn't yet understood that we all have to work for our success, one difficult step at a time.

Simple Cures for Loneliness

Loneliness is on the rise. The most recent US data studied by John Cacioppo, a social neuroscientist at the University of Chicago, found that almost a quarter of people today are plagued by frequent loneliness, regardless of gender, race, or education levels. A 2010 AARP survey found that of the people age 45 and up who participated in their study, 35% reported chronic loneliness compared with 20% ten years ago.

This disturbing trend reflects the fact that increasing numbers of people are living alone, added to the decrease in people joining groups and organizations that in the past fostered a sense of community. Robert Putnam, Ph.D. from Harvard (*Bowling Alone*, 2001), puts the blame on the long-term decline in Americans' civic engagement. Boomers and those younger have been less likely to join churches or other groups that supported feelings of belonging to something meaningful. The fact that a person has hundreds if not thousands of "friends" on Facebook can actually make loneliness worse, because we seem to need to be in the presence of each others' bodies.

The hidden costs of this isolation are now linked to serious health problems such as depression, alcohol abuse, sleep disorders, chronic pain, anxiety, and even dementia and

Alzheimer's. The World Health Organization has rated lone-liness as a higher risk to health than smoking and as great a risk as obesity. Lonely people's immune systems become com-promised, increasing their risk of health problems, as well as their feelings of discouragement which affect their willingness to practice good self care.

Despite this epidemic, there appears to be a positive cor-relation between spirituality and lower reports of loneliness. In a study by Jacqueline Olds, M.D., people who identify as "very religious or spiritual" report half the degree of loneliness than people who identify as "not religious at all." People who attend religious or spiritual services once a month or more reported the lowest incidences of loneliness of all.

There is also a correlation between low reports of loneli-ness among people who donate their time to charities and other nonprofits. Volunteers who work together toward a common goal of helping others often develop meaningful relationships with each other.

It appears that spirituality is good for your physical, emo-tional, and relational health. Research indicates that the best prescription to prevent loneliness is to meet with others on a regular basis, join and become active in groups, volunteer for causes you believe in, and to put into action your understand-ing that we are all in this together.

More Than Sexy

The young woman sitting in front of me in my psychotherapy office is articulate, intelligent, well groomed and attractive. Jessica has also thrown up her food three times a day, every day, since puberty. "I have to be prettier," she says. "I just can't go on looking like this."

We might think Jessica's anxiety is all in her head, but a disturbing trend is leading to a different conclusion. A new study published in the journal *Sexuality and Culture* (September 2011) "has found that the portrayal of women in the media over the last several decades has become increasingly sexualized, even 'pornified,'" according to Erin Hatton, Ph.D., assistant professor at the University of Buffalo. "In the 2000's, there were 10 times more hypersexualized images of women than men... this is problematic because it indicates a decisive narrowing of media representations of women."

A report by the American Psychological Association's Task Force on the Sexualization of Girls (2007) found compelling evidence that the rise in sexualized images of girls and women in the media is harmful to their self-image and healthy maturation. This can mean undermining a woman's confidence in her body promoting shame, anxiety, eating disorders and/or depression. Sexualized images of women have been found to increase violence against them and to decreased sexual satisfaction among both sexes.

"The consequences of the sexualization of girls in media today are very real and are likely to be a negative influence on girls' healthy development," said Eileen Zurbriggen, Ph.D., chair of the Task Force and associate professor at UCSC. "As a society, we need to replace all of these sexualized images with ones showing girls in positive settings—ones that show the uniqueness and competence of girls… The goal should be to deliver messages to all adolescents, boys and girls, that lead to healthy sexual development."

As parents and other trusted adults, we play a major role in contributing to either the sexualization of the young women in our lives or to giving them a healthier sense of what it means to be a human being. We can take an educative role by encouraging young people to question the images that are being promoted and by sharing information on the negative effects.

Sexualization means that a person's value comes only from his/her sexual appeal to the exclusion of other characteristics. We can help young women like Jessica and all our daughters, nieces, friends, and yes, our young men, to understand that kindness, creativity, intellectual competence, physical abilities, compassion, service, spirituality and love matter more than being sexy.

Your Worst Nightmare

The gorgeous stranger across the room is returning your seductive smile. A warm glow and tingling sense of anticipation run through your body. The air seems electric, the atmosphere more alive. It's here!—love at first sight, irresistible attraction, the stuff movies are made of. The sexual chemistry is sizzling.

When that happens, run the other way as fast as you can, says Terry Gorski, noted addiction specialist. What we call "chemistry" is often not what we think. "Chemistry" can signal that a person who embodies your hurtful patterns in relationships has shown up again. In other words, the thrill you feel is an indication that you've just met your worst nightmare.

It's pretty much common knowledge at this point that the patterns for the partners we're looking for are set in childhood. The time-honored wisdom is that men marry their mothers, and women look for dear old dad. This could be a good thing, except when the family is a difficult one. Children who grow up in abusive homes, for example, often learn that love equals pain, because that's what they observe. When they grow up, even though they're smart and know better, the tattoo on their nervous system tells them that when they feel pain-equals-love, they're home.

If that sounds like your childhood environment, chances are good that you've been programmed to be attracted to the wrong thing. Many of my clients are single and don't want to be, and often I hear them say about perfectly nice people, "But I'm not attracted to her/him! I don't feel the chemistry!" Prioritizing "chemistry" might be exactly what is steering them wrong. We've all heard stories of people in the clutches of overwhelming attraction to practicing alcoholics, drug addicts, murderers on death row, and serial killers. It's a better bet in your search for a potential mate to prioritize sexy qualities like integrity, kindness, and generosity.

If you are one of the many who find yourself in recurring painful, problematic relationships, it may be news that you can enjoy feeling a chemical attraction with somebody hot but not have to have it mean anything more than that. Certainly, enjoy it! It's just not a reliable source for decision making. Through psychotherapy and/or other types of diligent work on yourself, it's possible to change the patterns of whom you are attracted to. It's about learning to use your brain as well as your heart and hormones.

Match.com University

Many of my single patients have lost sight of their humanity in the search for a beloved. Their list of criteria for a partner has become absurd. As soon as they meet someone who is as good looking as Brad and as sexy as Angelina, as rich as a Oprah and as unconditionally loving as the Dalai Lama, they will be able to let down their guard and love somebody.

I send them to Match.com not to find a partner, but for an education:

- A common complaint is "there's no one out there" or "all the good ones are taken." By browsing for free, you will find out how many prospects are actually out there. If you live in a major metropolitan area, there are a seemingly endless number of possible partners which will challenge those beliefs for good.

- Browsing will also confront the idea that online dating is only for nerds. When you see how many smart, attractive, accomplished, kindly people are online, you will change your mind. Statistics say that today one in five married couples met online.

- Match.com is a great place to get comfortable meeting friendly human beings. Spending time getting to

113

know other available people will help you remember that people are people before they are sex objects or arm candy, and will expose you to how decent and lovely most people are.

- The next step is "coffee dates." This is a meeting of about an hour in a public place such as Starbucks. You go on coffee dates with just about anyone who asks in order to practice your conversation skills and find out if a friendship might be possible. Go out as often as you can, until you are comfortable meeting and conversing with strangers. You could meet three new people a week or even three in an evening.

- The only thing you need to know after meeting someone is whether you'd like to see them again. It's too soon to know if you want to marry the person or have a baby. Most single people make up their minds too quickly, such as in the first few seconds.

- You'll come to accept that dating is basically a game of rejection—either you reject, or you get rejected. Learning not to take it personally will help with dating and with all of life.

Match.com has enough candidates looking for love for you to learn to how to meet and enjoy other human beings instead of waiting around for Mr/Ms Perfect. You can use what you learn at Match.com University to return kindness and humanity to the dating world.

Is There Such a Thing as Sex Addiction?

Steven is remembering the active days of what he calls his sex addiction: "I was at a party and noticed this overweight, not so beautiful woman across the room who was obviously attracted to me." He drums his fingers on the table. "I did my number on her and got her to go out to the barn behind the house where we had sex; then we went back inside to the party. Later, I remember I glanced over at her, and she was crying." He breaks eye contact and looks away. "It was sad because I knew I had hurt her, injured her self confidence, but who she was as a person had nothing to do with it. She was just *next*."

Steven is currently an active member of AA and Sex Addicts Anonymous (SAA). He's also in longterm therapy dealing with the fact that he's nearing fifty and has never sustained a relationship with a woman for longer than a year and never one that included his being monogamous. "It's all the same addiction," he says. "The drinking, the pot, the sex—it's all about not being able to really connect with anybody."

Whether or not such a thing as "sex addiction" exists is controversial. In *Why There is No Such Thing as Sex Addiction— and Why it Really Matters*, Dr. Marty Klein argues that by using such a phrase, we are at risk for pathologizing sexual behavior which is outside the mainstream. This is an important consideration, because society has a way of making people wrong who are sexually active and alive, people we might call "sex positive." The mainstream often makes people wrong who have a lot of partners, or people who engage in alternative lifestyles such as polyamory whether they have psychological problems or not. People may be branded as "sex addicts" just because they really, really like sex.

The point is that a person's sexual activity may or may not coexist with psychological problems. Many times people who prefer sexual behaviors outside the mainstream are completely psychologically healthy and certainly not "sex addicted." However, counselors of all types are seeing increasing numbers of clients with problematic sexual habits that are causing a great deal of pain. These might be addictions to Internet porn, compulsive masturbation, molestation, the compulsive pursuit and abandonment of sex partners, or infidelity. It is estimated by Dr. Patrick Carnes that 3-6% of the population meets the criteria for sex addiction.

One of the ways to tell the difference between healthy and unhealthy sexual activity is the degree to which a person feels out of control of their behavior, or that it hurts themself or other people. If something feels this way to you, find the help of a counselor or program who will not judge you and will help you continue your journey toward greater sexual health.

How Can You Feel Sexy When You're All Stressed Out?

Sure, I know, there's work, and working out, and eating right, and the economy, and relationship struggles, and, and, and... and then if you have kids, there's even more.

What a balancing act! Sometimes, it's a wonder we have any energy left for sex at all. To make sure it doesn't get that way for you, learn to become better at managing your stress. Here are some tips:

- Turn off your phone. The likelihood that there's going to be an emergency in the next hour is minuscule. If you can't hear it ringing, you'll be less likely to get involved in something that this is not the right time for.

- Cut down the amount of caffeine in your life. If you're really brave, do away with it all together.

- Relaxed breathing is full and deep. Stressed out breathing is short and shallow. Practice slowing your breathing and letting it fall all the way below your belly button, down to your genitals. There, doesn't that feel good? If smokers get to take smoke breaks, the rest of us are owed "breathing breaks."

117

- Use the Rule of Fifteen: Get up fifteen minutes earlier in the morning. The inevitable morning mishaps will be less irritating, and you'll get a good start to your day. Allow fifteen minutes of extra time to get to appointments. You'll feel in control, and everyone else will be impressed with your efficiency.

- Don't try to rely on your memory. Get a planner, and write everything down. This will help you get organized, always a good prevention method for fighting stress.

- Eliminate destructive self-talk such as "I'm too fat..." or "I'm too old..." Either argue with these nonsensical thoughts or get help from a therapist to eradicate them from your life. No one ever improved from being criticized to death.

- Allow time every day for yourself, for privacy, quiet, and introspection. If the only time for this is in the car, take full advantage of it. Even if it's only five minutes, if it's full and present and in the moment, your life will be enriched.

- Stretch periodically during the day. When you're at your job, especially if you sit for long periods of time, get up and walk once an hour. Stretch out your neck, your shoulders, and feel how good it is to be in your body.

- Talk it out. Discussing your situation with a trusted friend or with your lover can help clear your mind of confusion so you can concentrate on real problem solving.

- Learn to live one day at a time. If you live fully in the present moment, you'll find there's very little that needs to be changed.

The Seven Principles for Making Relationships Work

The Seven Principles for Making Marriage Work (Crown, 1999) is a book that I often recommend for people who are wishing to improve their relationships, married or otherwise. The author, Dr. John Gottman, actually hooked couples up to electrodes and watched what happened to their blood pressures and heart rates while they talked to each other. He found that he could predict with 91% accuracy whether their relationship was slated for the long term or headed for break-up.

Dr. Gottman found that even happily married people have screaming matches; the difference is in the way they argue. What is death to a relationship is treating your partner with criticism, contempt, defensiveness, or refusing to communicate.

Dr. Gottman's seven principles are:

1. Enhance Your Love Maps

Find out what works with your partner and do more of it.

2. Nurture Your Fondness and Admiration

Focus on what you like about your partner rather than their faults.

3. Turn Toward Each Other Instead of Away

One of the most destructive things you can do when things are going through a rough patch is to isolate and go off by yourself, leaving your partner alone to imagine the worst. Dr. Gottman found that couples with good relationships stick with their partner and turn toward each other, seeking solutions to their problems.

4. Let Your Partner Influence You

Dr. Gottman identified this as especially challenging for men: letting their partners influence them to share more vulnerability, to talk more about their feelings, and to not need to be in control all the time.

5. Solve Your Solvable Problems

Dr. Gottman says that 69% of the problems in any relationship will never be solved, so it is good to focus on the 31% that can be. Pick your battles. As they say in the AA prayer, "God, grant me the serenity to accept the things I cannot change, the courage to change the things I can, and the wisdom to know the difference."

6. Overcome Gridlock

Get whatever help you need to keep problems from backing up.

7. Create Shared Meaning

Examples of this would be to create new rituals around holidays and vacations.

Happily married people live an average of four years longer than those not so blessed and have been shown in test after test to have healthier immune systems, less chance of getting sick, and higher scores on happiness measures. To learn more about what you can do to improve your relationship, I would recommend this book to anyone. It is easy to read and has practical advice you can put into practice immediately.

The #1 Thing You Can Do to Improve Your Relationships

Feeling unappreciated is one of the main reasons people give for why they leave jobs and relationships. That's why it's so refreshing to hear what someone else appreciates about us. How nice is it to think of an oasis where someone is noticing what we do right.

The number one thing you can do today to improve your relationships is to tell someone what you appreciate about them. Not just a compliment like, "You look nice today" although under the right circumstances that's always good. The trick is to use the word "appreciate" because that's what people are starving for, being appreciated. It is actually better if you notice a small thing because it is unexpected, and the person gets to feel that you are noticing and approving of them.

Simple examples might be, "I appreciate that you took our son to the ball game." "I appreciate that you take time for yourself which allows me to do the same." "I appreciate that you take out the garbage before you're asked."

Mark and Diane were seeing me for marriage counseling because they were fighting and criticizing each other bitterly. I asked Mark to change gears and tell his wife something he appreciated about her. Diane waited nervously while Mark struggled to identify something, as this was a new way for him to think. When he finally said, "I appreciate that you dress so well for work," she broke out into a huge smile that looked as if he had given her a dozen roses. She hadn't known Mark was even paying attention.

Give it a try. Let your significant other off the hook and tell him or her a small thing you appreciate. Call your mother and give her "an appreciation." Let your employee know that you appreciate that she is always on time. Everyone can use a dose. Give someone the gift of appreciation today and watch your relationships blossom.

What's Your Love Language?

What makes one person feel loved is not always the same thing that makes another person feel loved. According to Gary Chapman in *The Five Love Languages* (Northfield Publishing, Chicago: 1995), there are five basic ways a person can communicate loving feelings to someone else, and our way is often not the same for someone we love. We are essentially speaking different languages. No matter how much we may tell someone we love them, if it is not in their "love language," they won't feel it.

The Five Love Languages are:

Words of Affirmation: Everyone likes to hear what they are doing right. Kind words, encouragement, compliments—these are perceived as signs of love especially by those with this as their primary love language. Often, we focus on "constructive criticism" or pointing out what we think the other person should change, which is far less effective than praise.

Quality Time: Quality time doesn't just mean spending enough time together, although that is a good start. It means time when we give our partner our undivided attention. It requires listening, not interrupting, and learning to talk about feelings.

Receiving Gifts: Gifts are a time-honored sign of love. If this is your partner's main love language, find ways to give tokens of affection frequently. Certainly tangible gifts are nice, but don't forget the gift of attention.

Acts of Service: This love language is often taken for granted. Help around the house, giving a backrub, cleaning up, taking the car to be washed—there are so many ways to express affection by doing service for someone else.

Physical Touch: This love language gets mixed up with sex all the time. Instead, it means expressing love by affectionately touching the body, stroking, patting, and holding hands. It means holding someone while they cry.

The idea with learning these "love languages" is that it will help tremendously if we identify which is our primary language and which is the language of our partner, then try to let our partner know they are loved in the way they are most likely to receive it. It may feel awkward at first but if we are persistent, we will see remarkable change. The more our partner feels loved, the more the good feelings will be returned and everybody wins.

Although Dr. Chapman does not cover this in his book, we can also win by learning to express our love in all five "languages." As we expand in our capacity for love and the ability to be loving to the world around us, we can express ourselves in all five ways and not live in a world where it has to be only our way.

Six Ways to Help a Woman
Get in the Mood

First of all, do not ask her if she wants to have sex. This question will go straight to her head, which is not where you want to be.

Second, long before you want to have sex, let her know how much you like her body. Start complimenting her the day before, the week before, better yet, make it a constant thing. In this culture where advertising and magazines are constantly telling us we are not measuring up, all women are insecure about their attractiveness. You would not believe the gorgeous fashion models I have had in my office who are obsessed with the idea that they are not beautiful enough. Make your compliments real and frequent. Work at it.

Third, realize that foreplay starts hours before sex. Spend some quality time giving her your full attention. Talking, cuddling, being physically close without (yet) being sexual, these things help a woman realize she might be in the mood. Mostly, it is about listening to her feelings and thoughts. One of the most aphrodisiac things for a woman to hear is, "Tell me more about that."

Fourth, focus on what is right with her and the relationship rather than what, in your opinion, is missing. If she thinks you prefer women who look or act like porn stars, she will have trouble opening herself to you. If you are critical of her body, her feelings, or her habits, why should she trust you by becoming more vulnerable? You've heard that old saying that you catch more flies with honey than vinegar, right? Tell her what you like, even if you need to stretch.

Fifth, you probably won't get much action if you don't do your fair share of the household duties. Not helping causes resentment (not a sexy emotion), and women consistently rate this as a primary reason for dissatisfaction in a relationship. If you're not up to it, neither is she. Spring for a housekeeper and watch her receptiveness increase.

Finally, don't wait to initiate sex until right before bed. She'll turn you down because she's too tired. Go to bed at least a half an hour early. If you're not ready to fall asleep afterwards, you can always get up to watch the tube or go online.

Good luck. Enjoy learning to seduce your partner. Won't you feel masterful when she melts like butter in your hands? Not only your relationship but the whole world will benefit from your increased pleasure and contentment.

Chapter 5

Tantric Fusion

The Body, Streaming Joy

When pent-up emotional trauma gets released in psycho-therapy, it's a giant upheaval to the entire system—physically, emotionally, mentally and spiritually. The release changes lives for the better, of course. All that secret, shameful, repressed garbage can finally be put out with the trash. A deep sense of relief and of lightness follows from not having to carry around the burden any longer.

It can be a great help during or after the time period when this cleaning-out is going on to have a series of sessions with an experienced bodyworker, in addition to the regularly sched-uled psychotherapy. Talk therapy alone is sufficient to release enough of the repressed material for major improvements to be experienced, but for a more complete resolution, bodywork can assist the process by working on it physically as well as intrapsychically.

The repressed material does not exist only in the mind or the heart. It has been lodged in the body: in the tissues, the organs, the muscles, and the fascia that connect the muscles to the bones. Trauma, whether emotional, physical or sexual, can show up in the body as poor postural alignment, stiffness, lack of flexibility, or as more serious health problems. When the bodyworker skillfully eases the physical release of this holding in the body, the result is often a whole new way of being in the world.

Rolfing is one such bodywork discipline that changes the structural problems resulting from trauma. I have personally found it to be highly effective. Once, when the Rolfer was working on my foot, it suddenly began kicking on its own, expelling anger that was trapped in it. I found myself literally "putting my foot down." In another session, I began crying with relief as he worked on my spine. The greatest surprise of all was the session when trapped joy that I never knew was there was released and began streaming out into the world.

Other forms of bodywork that can be useful during therapy are acupuncture, chiropractic, the Alexander Technique, Reiki, and Feldenkrais. Receiving a massage is a necessity for those folks who have not been touched enough, which is nearly everyone in the Western world. Of course, it's always helpful to take up a physical practice, such as running, hatha yoga, martial arts training, dancing, or even walking around the block. It's wonderful to explore the myriad methods of enhanced physical awareness that can bring levels of well being you had never imagined for yourself.

The Disciplines of Pleasure

The word "discipline" is most often attached to things we don't want to do. We don't want to exercise and we don't want to eat right; therefore "discipline" seems like a bummer. Our idea of a well-disciplined person is close to that of a military recruit: rigid and tense, running his or her life like clockwork. It can seem that being well disciplined is saying a big "no" to life.

Hedonism, on the other hand, or the devotion to pleasure, is considered the opposite of discipline. We all pretty much agree on what is pleasurable: bad-for-you foods, beverages, and activities. As Mark Twain once said, "Too much whiskey is barely enough." The American way of hedonism is that if something is pleasurable, then more would be better.

Neither is true. One must discipline oneself in order to experience pleasure more frequently and more often. For example, you've probably figured out that you prefer drinking less alcohol than you did in college because you don't want the hangovers, decidedly un-fun. Drinking is certainly pleasurable; most people have decided it's more so in moderation. Delicious food is more pleasurable in small quantities, because then you can also enjoy the pleasure of a fit body rather then the anti-pleasures of obesity, diabetes, and heart disease. Many people who refuse discipline find themselves unable to experience pleasure due to sickness or malaise and enervation.

I was taught by one of my early tantra teachers that "pleasure requires constant vigilance." True hedonism requires discipline, because one must exercise mindful awareness of what will ultimately contribute to pleasure.

We can develop a practice of incorporating daily pleasurable experiences for the body. We're lucky in urban areas that massages, Jacuzzis, saunas, manicures and pedicures are affordable treats for women and men. We can practice looking at beauty in our many vistas of nature, or in the wonderful art museums (which all have free admission on certain days). We can hike in the hills, go for a swim, or exchange affection with a loved one. If we fail to discipline ourselves to take our pleasure seriously, we are prone to compulsively seek to fulfill this need through addictive pleasures. In other words, if we don't seek pleasure consciously, we will demand it in unconscious and unhealthy ways.

Many spiritual people try to deny their need for pleasure and deprive themselves, believing asceticism is the way to god. They think of the spiritual path as one of self denial, fasting, weird restrictive diets, and forcing disciplines on themselves that they don't want and which may even be harmful. I would like to suggest that the spiritual path can be the most pleasurable of all—full of the disciplined pleasure of a great "yes" to life.

Better Than Average Body Maintenance is Required

If you want to develop beyond the mainstream, you'll have to be willing to do beyond what the mainstream does. If you look around at the 70% of Americans who are overweight, you'll know that you simply cannot eat what everyone else is eating or participate in the health-ruining practices advocated by advertising. If you eat as you have been taught in this culture, you will be in a stupor and not able to participate in higher levels of consciousness.

You will also have to willingly participate in a disciplined program of exercise. Hatha yoga was developed in the East as a method for spiritual seekers to train their bodies for maximum spirituality, and as we know, it has become popular in the West. It is not necessarily superior to "Western yoga:" working out at the gym, lifting weights, running, and sports. There are also forms of exercise that support more esoteric forms of energy flow such as Tai Chi, Pilates, martial arts, and dance.

The point of all this body discipline is better health, of course, but it is primarily to increase awareness of the body. In the majority of people in Western culture, their awareness stops at the neck. They may experience sensation in their genitals or when the body is in pain, but that's about it. They are not even aware that they are not aware. So mindfulness exercises such as progressive relaxation can be beneficial as well.

It's not necessary to be in optimum physical health, or to have a chiseled physique, or be more than average good looking. People with disabilities have the same needs for above average body discipline. When you maintain your body like a well-oiled machine, it will cause minimal trouble, be a pleasurable place to live, and increase your awareness beyond just your mind.

Most people in this culture are completely identified with the content of their minds. They believe that what they are thinking is true and have never questioned it. When you start to develop body awareness, you will know without doubt that there are other ways of knowing beyond the mind. You may come to trust your heart and the wisdom of the body far more than what your mind is telling you.

What's All This Talk About Cleansing?

People can get really crazy with this stuff, but it does benefit you to cleanse your body from time to time. Body purification processes are good to learn about and practice. The idea is that we all have stuff that has not been completely eliminated which clogs up our bodies and our colons and needs to come out. This blockage is partially due to the diets we eat today, which have everything to do with tasting good and little to do with nutrition, but also to the nature of things—things get dirty and need to be cleaned.

It's as if you never cleaned your house or your car, and all that gunk kept building up. When you go on a cleanse and release old toxic matter that has been in you for decades, you will also release the emotions that have been trapped. The toxic matter often contains the energy of what was going on that we held onto, sometimes sadness, or anger, or other emotional stuckness that needs release. All this trapped stuff inside is toxic build-up; it affects your emotions and makes your attitude negative. Concurrent psychotherapy can be very helpful with the release process.

Spring ("spring cleaning") or summer when the weather is hot are the best times to go on a cleanse. Most involve eating lighter on the food chain, or eating only alkaline foods, or fasting, plus eliminative herbs. Most involve cleansing processes like colonics and/or enemas. You have to get over your distaste for this; it will be good for your acceptance of your and other people's bodies. The main teaching on a tantric level is getting over your revulsion to the body's natural processes.

Personally, I love the Arise & Shine program and have done it at least a dozen times. It involves eating only fruits, vegetables, and alkaline grains plus herbs for a month, and then if you're ready, fasting on juice and water for an intensive week. You learn a lot about your body when you see how much stuff comes out of you when you're not eating. I mean, where is that stuff coming from? Gross, but certainly it is better out of the body than in.

When you are cleaned out, you will experience new levels of clarity, well being, and health. For a while, you will have lost your cravings for addictive foods, but only until you start eating them again. You will bring to yourself and all you meet a new clean, shining awareness without all that toxicity standing between you.

The Eight Levels of Human Development

Timothy Leary is remembered by many as a drug-crazed hippie freak, but he was a serious psychologist and passionate seeker of freedom for the exploration of the human mind. *Exo-Psychology* is an important book he wrote which posited 8 levels of human development. When I read it, it was the first time I had seen Western ideas about higher functioning, and ones that did not necessarily include hours of meditation a day. The East had long talked about higher levels of functioning but not the West. We were stuck with adjusting to the mainstream as the goal, which for many people, it is not.

The first four levels in *Exo-Psychology*, Levels I-IV, are about mastering the ability to function in the world, a topic well covered by mainstream psychology. The levels are about mastering survival, basic emotional functioning and social skills enough to be successful in the work world. These levels are essential before one can move on to the last four levels, which are where it gets really interesting:

Level V: The stage of identifying as a bodymind, becoming a master of the body. Bodily disciplines such as nutrition and exercise, increasing flexibility, subtle energies, awareness of breath, as well as disciplined hedonism, the sexual arts, tantric fusion with one's partner. Learning the value of relaxing and enjoying, being high and "floating."

Level VI: The ability to achieve brain mastery: You don't have to believe what you think. Your brain can be dialed, tuned, and focused to create new realities. You learn to control your brain, rather than your thoughts being controlled by the mass culture or the non-helpful programming of your parents.

Level VII: The stage of evolutionary consciousness, or the understanding that you have a role as an evolutionary agent. That your work on yourself serves all beings. Awareness of Jung's "collective unconscious."

Level VIII: The stage of spirituality, awakening of kundalini, illumination, out-of-body experiences, mysticism. This, says Leary, is the highest state of development available to all, not just mystics in caves in India.

Of course, Leary was an advocate of using drugs to experience and evolve into these Levels. Since he published the book in the late 70s, people have been actively developing drug-less methods. It's wonderful to have these guidelines for how we might remain useful to society while we are developing ourselves to the farthest reaches possible.

You Can Induce Bliss at Any Moment

People think that bliss states are dependent on buying and owning the right things, being in the right environment, finding a sexy partner, or years of spiritual discipline. The truth is, bliss states are available to you any time, anywhere.

Such as right now. Walk with me through this technique I developed when I lived in India:

- **Unfocused Eyes** As I've written before, the aggressive Western gaze reaches out and claims the environment, penetrating, owning, criticizing, and conquering. When we unfocus the eyes, they become soft and open to receive.

- **Be Breathed** Slow your breathing down, all the way down. Notice the difference between when you are doing the breathing, such as when purposefully take a deep breath, and when the breathing is happening by itself. Are you breathing? No, "something" or "someone" is breathing you. Enjoy being breathed: No effort is required.

- **All the Way to the Root** In the modern world, we breathe rapidly and shallowly, with the breath staying at the top of the chest. If you look at statues of the Buddha, he has a big fat belly, symbolizing that his breath was so relaxed it went all the way into his abdomen. Bring the breath down to your tailbone. Let it push out your belly when it inhales, then deflate like a balloon during the exhale.

- **Watch the Flow** Feel the breath flowing in and out by itself, over and over. Observe it circulating all the way down, up and out. If you are somewhere there is activity, open to the flow of humanity or nature with your unfocused eyes. If your mind starts its endless judgment, watch that, too.

- **Blissfulness** Become aware that blissfulness is happening. It may not be as dramatic as you have been led to believe, but there it is, flowing within you at all times, below the level of your awareness, just waiting for you to tune into its frequency. It's not anything you need to search for—it's been there all along.

This technique might be easiest to learn and practice lying silently in a quiet room, but you can practice on a busy city street, in a Board meeting, or during an argument with your lover. These are more challenging situations, of course, but the point of any meditation practice is to bring these higher states into our daily lives.

The Eyes, Your False Friends

I often send my single patients to Starbucks to sit and people watch in a different way than they are used to. I ask them to scan for people who look kind, responsible, trustworthy: the type of person, for example, who thinks it would be fun to coach Little League after work. People often get all tangled up in their love lives because the kind of person who would make a good parent to their future kids does not look like the person who fuels their erotic fantasies.

Back when I was studying tantra in India, we did many of our exercises blindfolded. When we couldn't see, we learned to read the information our bodies were giving us about a person, such as whether or not they could be trusted, whether or not their energy was compatible with ours. Experimenting in such an environment of trust and vulnerability, we all fell in love with each other regardless of whom our eyes might have prejudged as unworthy.

The way the advertising industry spends billions to convince us that only people who look a certain way are desirable may be related to alarming new statistics about a 60% increase in reports of chronic and crippling loneliness. We are endlessly encouraged to focus on abs and sexiness, not on whether a person would make a good friend or partner. Some of the images selling perfume are down right frightening—if you look closely enough, several of the male models, although conventionally good looking, have the menacing stare of a rapist.

The reports back from Starbucks are that this practice is revolutionary. For many of the clients who come to me lonely and wishing they were partnered, their eyes have become their false friends, encouraging them to search in a way that can't bring them happiness. Osho, the great tantra master, once said, "If you are alone and lonely, it is only because you have too many criteria on your love."

Even if you're not concerned with dating or finding a partner, consider how relying primarily on your eyes for information might be keeping you from more fully exploring smell, touch, sound, and taste. Closing your eyes, getting out of the realm of the visual, is one of the most transformative practices you could take up. In the same way that silence can be the most beautiful sound of all, not seeing in the way you've been trained to see could offer you unexpected vision.

Friends or Lovers: Do We Have to Choose?

John Gottman, Ph.D., is considered today's leading researcher on what makes relationships work. He actually hooks couples up to electrodes and measures them when they argue and talk. Dr. Gottman claims he can predict with 91% accuracy whether a couple will make it after chatting with them for fifteen minutes.

This fact from his research seems to surprise everyone: 70% of both men and women rate the quality of the friendship as the most important thing in a successful relationship. People are surprised because the media portrays men as so sexually fixated that they assume sex is their highest value, however, not so according to Dr. Gottman. This supports the idea that anything couples can do to enhance their friendship will increase longevity and greater degrees of happiness and satisfaction.

On the other hand, David Deida, another of today's relationship gurus, believes that friendship between men and women kills sexual attraction. He believes sexual attraction is based on mystery, otherness and the masculine/feminine polarity; and that friendship neutralizes all that. Deida teaches that what women truly want is to be ravished, which sounds misogynistic because men are supposed to ravish women and women are supposed to surrender to it, until you consider that romance novels are all about this and are the best-selling genre of books.

I met a therapist who formerly worked with David Deida and currently has a private practice specializing in seeing clients who have been damaged by his work, particularly women. Many others have been helped, however. His controversial ideas resonate with many well-educated, outside-the-mainstream people.

The latest expert on the scene is Esther Perel, author of *Mating in Captivity: Reconciling the Erotic and the Domestic.* She adds fuel to the fire by writing, "The very ingredients that nurture love—mutuality, reciprocity, protection, worry, responsibility for the other—are sometimes the very ingredients that stifle desire."

A lot of people yearn for a lover who is their best friend. A friend of mine who's in a long-term relationship and will remain so, says that she and her partner are not friends; at least not in the way she is with her girlfriends. He thinks they're best friends, but she would never talk with him the way she feels free to talk with a woman.

I don't have the answer. Do you want to be friends with your lover? The debate continues.

The Egg Meditation

I invented The Egg Meditation after reading *Becoming a Woman* by Dr. Toni Grant. The book was the first time I encountered the idea that as women we are losing our yin. Dr. Grant never used that language, but as a Jungian she taught that humans are made up of different components or subpersonalities, and that as modern women, we are emphasizing our active "doing" parts at the expense of our quiet "being" parts. Today, women are busy expressing our assertiveness: becoming CEO's, stripping for our lovers, and being on top. We reject what has classically been considered female: being quiet, receptive, and demure. We're all yang and no yin.

When I took sex education in high school, we were shown the most amazing video of an egg being impregnated by a sperm. There She sat, unmoving, glowing, queenly, radiating, waiting patiently in all her splendor. The sperm were wriggling and squirming and jockeying for position, all of them anxious to enter Her. One victorious little tadpole finally succeeded. The egg didn't move a muscle, and, except for a little squeal of ecstasy when he entered, appeared unmoved by the whole experience.

The old fashioned way of pursuit was reportedly like this: Men pursued women who were non-active. Men did all the work. Then, during the radical changes of the 70s, Germaine Greer exhorted women to take the lead and pursue whichever men we wanted—it seemed like a good idea at the time. Men and women should certainly do whatever is right for their personal temperament. Nevertheless, neither modern men nor women have any connection to their yin self.

I took some time and meditated on the Egg, imagining myself as Her: sitting silently, radiating, waiting. After practicing a few times, I took it on the road. Since I used to be socially shy, I'd never been approached all that much in bars, so as usual, I sat and watched all the hotties move on each other. I closed my eyes there on my barstool and did my Egg Meditation, envisioning myself as the Queen Egg, glowing, unmoving, and calm. When I opened my eyes, much to my surprise, several attractive men had wriggled up, jockeying for position. I was never approached as much in all my life as that night.

Yang is looking for yin, sorely missing in today's world. I'm not advocating that women give up the gains we've made, not by a long shot. But both men and women are missing the element of yin. That's why some men think they want younger or submissive women. Most modern men don't really want submissive; they want a worthy partner. But yang is looking for yin and not more yang. There has to be a balance.

So just for a few minutes, imagine... you're the queen Egg, sitting unmoving... getting fully in touch with your feminine side.

The Yin of Sex, Part One

Pole dance classes at your local "Y," burlesque and striptease billed as "female empowerment," fetish shoes as ordinary daywear, cougars on the prowl, and porn star sex not only ubiquitous on the Internet but expected in every bedroom—contemporary sex is all about the yang.

You've seen the yin/yang symbol: the white and black teardrops coexisting inside a circle, each half complimenting the other, each essential for the other's existence. In the East, the timeless symbol demonstrates that all in the manifest world exists as a pair of opposites: fast/slow, hot/cold, passive/aggressive, male/female. These opposites exist only in relation to each other, creating a world of perfect balance.

In terms of sex, yang is outer directed (like a penis): aggressive, hot, noisy, fast, focused on technique, and headed toward the goal of orgasm. Sex is often voyeuristic, a spectator sport, with a preference for the visual. In prior times, yang was the sole province of men, the masculine.

Yin sexuality is the opposite: inner directed (like a vagina): passive, cool, slow, quiet, meandering, with no other goal than shared sensuality. Yin is full of secrets, soft, yielding, private, hidden, shy and reticent. Women, the feminine, were

151

the sole holders of yin.

Women in the sexist past had no choice but to embody yin, or men yang, with dire consequences for those who strayed from their stereotypes. Most people of today enjoy our potential for greater flexibility and the openness toward people of all persuasions. Ideally, both men and women would embrace their inner yin as well as their outer yang, but that is not what is happening.

Yin is no longer an option anywhere in the West, including the bedroom. Women are boldly exhibiting their yang qualities—nobody wants to be seen as weak. We are prejudiced against the slow, the soft, the passive, the diffuse, the meandering, the unfocused, the yielding. Self-help books and seminar leaders encourage eradicating any yin qualities in oneself in order to be always assertive, bold, virile. Porn promotes a preference for yang sex. We devalue the yin, both in ourselves and others, which is misogyny in a subtle, insidious form.

It is a timeless truth that both yin and yang are essential, and that everything and everyone carry both qualities. It doesn't help to repress or pretend you don't have yin. If you do, you will never know yourself. The next time you notice you are feeling shy, or reticent, or passive, or slow, that you don't feel like sharing, or that you want sex that explores aimlessly and doesn't go anywhere, instead of finding it wrong, you begin a fascinating exploration of what this hidden part of yourself is all about.

The Yin of Sex, Part Two

The adorable young woman sitting in front of me has been sent by her boyfriend for counseling because she doesn't orgasm in a few minutes as a porn star pretends to.

The main source of sex education for many young people these days is online porn, and much misinformation is being disseminated. The major inaccuracy is that yang sex is all there is: sex is only about looking a certain way, vigorous activity, technique, and performance. There is no place for sensual exploration, non-goal oriented play, or relaxation in the presence of the beloved. Very few even get the opportunity to learn that yin sex exists.

When a man and a woman can be totally themselves in each other's presence, a whole other dimension opens up. When I was studying tantra in India, we spent much of our time doing exercises to get over our fears of the opposite sex and learning to be emotionally real with each other. It wasn't about performance. It was about learning to take it slow, slower, and slowest.

Osho, the great tantra master, talks about an unknown-to-the-West phenomena, "valley orgasms." These are the opposite of the yang orgasms that end with a bang or, as Osho says, like a sneeze. A "valley orgasm" occurs from surrendering so deeply with the partner that an inner explosion happens.

"There are two types of climaxes, two types of orgasm. One type of orgasm is known. You reach to a peak of excitement, then you cannot go further: the end has come…In the second, excitement is just a beginning. And once the man has entered, both lover and beloved can relax. No movement is needed. They can relax in a loving embrace.

"When the man feels or the woman feels that the erection is going to be lost, only then is a little movement and excitement required. But then again relax. You can prolong this deep embrace for hours with no ejaculation… You may not be aware of it, but this is a fact of biology, of bio-energy, that man and woman are opposite forces. Negative-positive, yin-yang, they are challenging to each other. And when they both meet in a deep relaxation, they revitalize each other." (Osho, 1998, *The Book of Secrets*, NY: St Martin's Griffin.)

Once you become honest in your sexuality, both the yin and the yang of it, you will be able to enjoy the performance aspect of sex without being trapped in it. Sometimes, you will act the porn star and use all the fabulous techniques you've learned (that everyone else has learned, too), and other times you will experiment with your soft, flowing yin nature. You will be free to be alternately passive or aggressive, hot or not, and able to admit when increased intimacy scares you. You will be sexually real and not have to fake orgasms like a porn star.

154

What Do We Mean by "Spiritual Relationships?"

"WIIFM" is the primary motivator for many people in their relationships. WIIFM is a marketing term for "What's In It For Me?" We have been taught to value people for how good they will look on our arm, how close they come to our fantasy of the ideal lover, or how we imagine they will fulfill our desires. It's about how it all looks, right? Except that when we focus on the outside, nobody is going to be good enough because everyone is flawed. Everybody. This is why we love the tabloids—we get to see seemingly perfect celebrities with their defects hanging out.

One characteristic of a spiritual relationship is that instead of focusing on the other person's exterior, we focus on the perfection within. Just as we all have not-so-beautiful parts on the outside, we all have a perfect core at our center. When we want our relationship to have a spiritual component, we attempt to keep our attention on this perfection within, rather concentrating on what's outside.

The great tantra master Osho once said regarding relationships, "The Other is always right." I was stunned when I first heard this. Like most people, I had been constantly pointing out when I was right and my partner was wrong, all in the name of "communicating honestly." In retrospect, it was all a thinly disguised power struggle.

I argued with Osho's statement in my mind and then decided to see what I could learn from it. As a technique, I recommend it highly. You don't have to agree with it to experiment. Practice interpreting that the other was right and you were wrong next time you are reviewing a fight or disagreement. The ego spends all its time proving that it is superior. See what happens from the perspective of love.

When you begin this discipline of seeing what is right about the other person rather than what is, according to you, wrong, you may start to experience your partner as your teacher, or guru. Some of the other attributes of spiritual relationships that people have mentioned are a placing a high value on listening, integrity, emotional openness, sensitivity, truth, having a raise-the-bar attitude, and having a passion for learning and growing.

When people's lives are dedicated to something higher than just getting their own needs met, their relationships will follow suit. This can show up as a dedication to make the world a better place by working for the environment, helping kids, or serving some other higher calling. Your relationship will be dedicated to something more important than merely trying to get your needs met, and this is what we call a spiritual relationship.

What's the Difference Between Sensuality and Sexuality?

Everybody knows what's sexy, right? We see images all the time of good-looking men and women, smoking physiques, and enticing faces. Every year *People* magazine tells us who is the Sexiest Man Alive! and men's magazines are full of images of alluring women. There is one standard of beauty offered, and a real human being's sexiness quotient is measured by how closely they measure up to the media's promotion of who and what are sexy.

In our culture, attraction has become an entirely visual experience. Instead of eroticizing the whole body, we make love with our eyes only. Our relationship to our own bodies has become one of working on them at the gym in order to be visually attractive to potential lovers, to the exclusion of anything else.

But the visual is only one of our five senses, and by telling us that the visual is what's sexy, we learn to have a skewed emphasis on physical image. We come to pay less attention to the other four senses, and the art of sensuality is being lost. When we talk about the sensual, we are talking about the seductive qualities of the sound of our lover's voice and the sighs of lovemaking, our partner's particular scent, the taste of their sweat, and the touch of their skin.

Sensual sex is about two people connecting through all five senses. We are meant to make love not only with our eyes, but also with our nose, our ears, our mouths, and our hands. We can learn to enjoy the touch, scent, sound, and taste of sex, instead of only the sight. Many of the exercises practiced in the art of tantra are conducted blindfolded to short-circuit the eyes and have the practitioner focus instead on the other senses.

There is a famous story of Napoleon writing home to his wife, Josephine, "I'll be home in three days. Don't bathe." To men of an earlier generation, the natural scent of a woman was an intoxicating aphrodisiac that drove them wild with desire.

Sensual means that you appreciate your partner in his or her entirety, experiencing their desirability just the way they are. Rather than focusing on what, in your opinion, is not like a magazine cover, close your eyes and feel, listen, smell, and touch the incredible sexiness of this particular lover who is gracing you with their intimacy and vulnerability. Every person wants to be loved in their totality, not as just a collection of body parts.

Sex as Roto-Rooter

Sex is fun. Well… isn't it? Sometimes it is, for sure. At least the kind in the movies is—performed by perfect bodies, smooth and satisfying. The kind porn promotes is—partners always willing, available, with no emotions at all, let alone difficult ones. You know, the kind of sex you imagine everyone else is having: fun and trouble-free.

Then there's the kind of sex we don't talk about much: the kind that dredges up your insecurities, fears of intimacy, of letting go or losing control. It brings up your shame that your body doesn't measure up: your boobs are too small or lopsided; your dick isn't big enough. Sex can reveal to you your lack of trust in the people closest to you, or your performance fears. It can force you to confront abuse issues long buried or forgotten.

This unearthing of hidden issues is not normally seen as the purpose of sex, but metaphysically, it is. Sex can function as a transformative mechanism to unearth, like a Roto-Rooter, your unfinished business so you will explore and grow and evolve. If you stay in the mainstream mindset that sex is only supposed to be fun, you will miss its healing potential.

Most of us, when this uncomfortable stuff emerges, rush

to push it back down. This defeats the very reason it came up in the first place—for us to deal with our issues and clean them out. Some, maybe most, people think that when these issues arise, it's a problem and wrong, and they will do anything not to share them with their partners. The prevalent message is that you are not supposed to be having all this insecurity. If you do, somehow, it is supposed to magically disappear when you get undressed and into bed with someone.

People who suffered childhood sexual abuse, one in three women and one in ten men, are particularly prone to being exposed to the healing potential of sex. But all of us have been sexually traumatized in some way, such as by too early exposure to porn, overly sexual billboards, and the many ways contributing to the oversexualization of girls. For people healing from abuse, sex can be troublesome, not easy, and not particularly fun. They may benefit from seeking help from a therapist who understands how to help.

Basically, there are three kinds of sex: the fun sensual kind that some people are having and everyone else is pretending they're having. There's the kind that has the spiritual purpose of forcing you to grow by tunneling deep into the inner recesses of your psyche to solve your psychological issues. The third kind is transcendent, spiritual sex, in which you melt and dissolve into your partner and the cosmos.

The Quickest Route to Tantric Sex

Tantra is about making love into an art. If you thought of yourself as an artist of love, what would you create? If you were painting a picture of the most juicy, delicious, perfect afternoon with your beloved, composing a song, or sculpting a masterpiece, how would you honor them?

Tantric lovers take their time. They are not in a hurry. Tantra has everything to do with savoring the moment, and bringing awareness to every detail. Noticing what you've never noticed before. Did you ever consider that the inside of the elbow could be an erogenous zone? That you can turn on your partner by tickling the small of his or her back?

The quickest route to tantric sex is to slow down, wa-a-a-ay down. Do everything you normally do, but twice or even three times slower than usual. Focus at first on anything and everything but the genitals. Slow. Slowly. Uhmmmm, painfully, agonizingly slow.

As leisurely as you've ever touched anyone, stroke down the inside of her thigh in the most languorous motion possible. Brush his nipples with your palm with a touch as light as a peacock feather. Your hand slides down his side so slowly that its movement would be imperceptible to an observer, as if you weren't even moving. When you take as much time as you've ever wanted to lick, swirl, and savor, the taste of your beloved's lips is divine. Pleasure him or her with the slow Chinese water torture of your touch.

Think of your gratitude for this moment, for your lover, for being able to express your celebration through your hands. Each moment is precious and sacred if you only pay attention. Be meditative, intimate; prolong the act of love.

Sting once told reporters that he and his wife, Trudie, practiced tantric sex for up to four hours at a time. He later explained that this time frame included their flirtation, having dinner, getting undressed, and sexual play as all a part of tantric lovemaking. In tantra, these activities are not seen as "foreplay," but rather as opportunities for awareness and sensual pleasure; they are not less than intercourse itself.

Even if you think you are bored with this partner, with their body, approach it as if you've never been with it before. Watch with your awareness how much you can learn about pleasing a body you thought you knew. Enjoy your lover responding in ways you've never experienced before. How could anyone ever not be in the mood if every time were exquisitely different, shimmering with awareness? In tantric lovemaking, the quickest route is the slowest.

Envisioning Your Lover as the God or Goddess They Truly Are

One tantric exercise you can practice at home is to envision your lover as the god or goddess they truly are. That may seem a bit farfetched in today's world, as modern lovers are well too aware of what is "wrong" with their partner. Constantly bombarded with images of what the perfect lover looks like, talks like, kisses like, and makes love like, we compare and analyze and find our partners not measuring up. Since it is hard for a mere human being to live up to these two-dimensional fantasy figures, most of us experience our lovers (and ourselves) as lacking in the love department.

But what if we didn't focus on what we thought was wrong, but on what is right? What if we imagined the real person underneath their skin and their annoying habits? What if we pictured our beloved as their essential nature and allowed ourselves to honor their lovingness, their vulnerability, and their attempts at becoming a better person?

When we imagine our partner as whole and perfect instead of fragmented and flawed, it becomes impossible to abuse, degrade, or dehumanize the other person. If they are by definition an equal, we cannot cultivate a condescending, contemptuous attitude. On the contrary, we view them with the gaze of a deity who is one of tenderness, clarity, and passion. Seeing our self as whole and perfect, our partner becomes a mirror of that perfection.

Ancient Tantric Buddhists practiced seeing the man as a male Buddha and the woman as a female Buddha; and therefore, lovemaking became two Buddhas making love. The lovers practiced seeing each other as pure energy spontaneously expressing itself in embodied being.

Today, you can have fun with these practices. Certain tantric gods and goddesses had red or blue skin that could be fun to imagine. Some tantric texts describe the body of the lover as translucent or luminous like a rainbow. Think how delightful this could be to envision while stroking your lover's skin!

The tantrikas saw their feelings of passion and desire as having a transcendent aspect, and their mutual attraction as ultimately motivated by a spiritual impulse toward ecstasy. To move in the direction of an attitude like this can help transform the negative messages most of us were brought up with concerning sex. By envisioning our beloved as divine, it is possible to increase the love in the world and to elevate our ordinary sex acts to acts of worship.

Chapter 6

Creating Our Reality—At Least The Part We Can

The Bossa Nova Cure

"When I'm listening to bossa nova, it seems as if everything's right with the world." I was talking to my therapist of the time about my (then) chronic depression. I hadn't been seeing him that long, and we were still finding out if it was a fit. "That slinky slide," I said, "that bittersweet quality, that sexy smooth sunlight-on-the-beach thing. You get the feeling that whatever happens with the world, it'll be okay." I looked to see if he was tracking. "It's practically a spiritual thing."

The therapist was looking at me intently. His hair was graying, and mine wasn't. At least not obviously. "You've just named your cure," he said. "Listen to more bossa nova."

You'd be amazed to find out how many of my depressed patients subsist on a diet of Morrissey and The Cure. Or the anxious ones who live on the most aggro Hip Hop and several grande Starbucks a day. A client I once had to intervene on so she wouldn't kill herself? Her favorite band was the Suicidal Tendencies. (She came back the next week wearing a T-shirt she had made that said, "Choose Life.") (Not knowing that that usually means something else.)

The other day I caught myself cursing at a #$%& driver on the freeway. When I came to, I noticed I was all adrenal-ized by the *The World of Goa Trance* I was listening to. Well, no wonder. I switched to *Love, Peace, Chant* by David Newman. The other drivers on the road sighed a silent "thank you."

I'm not a trained music therapist, but it seems to me there's a lot to be said for orchestrating the soundtrack of our lives. It's alchemy, yes? A little of this, a little of that, until we get just the right mood.

Sometimes, psychotherapy is really helpful. Nothing matches it for getting unstuck, extricating ourselves from ancient patterns we can't see on our own. Sometimes, we really need that other person in our court, someone who has already delved into realms we're only beginning to explore. Other times, what we need is a lifestyle overhaul, like some new music. Bossa Nova may not be your thing, but what if it is, and you've been missing out all this time? Or it might be African music, which is a dependable mood lifter, as well. Choose more of what makes you happy. Really happy, not just addictively high. There's a big difference, you know.

I didn't stay with that therapist very long, but from that one simple directive I gained more than from others I stayed with for years. You should see my bossa nova collection. *Getz/ Gilberto*, anyone?

Turning On the Light in the Basement

Sometimes in therapy, it can feel as if you're going backward instead of making progress. Sometimes, it might appear that you're much sicker than you thought. Well, you might be, but then again, you probably aren't. It's just that when you finally catch a glimpse of all the stuff you've been avoiding, you may be shocked at what you see.

It's like turning on a light and going down into the basement: You had no idea that it's so dirty, full of cobwebs, dust, and dirt. But nothing's new—it's been that way for years. You've gotten used to the way it is and hadn't realized so much had built up.

Actually, it's a sign of progress to be willing to see the truth of it. When you face how messy it's become, you and your therapist can get in there and straighten it out. If we hadn't turned on the light and seen what's what, we wouldn't be able to move forward in our work of tossing out old rubbish, deciding what to keep and what not, and taking out the trash once and for all.

We've all seen horror movies where we shout at the heroine, "You fool! Don't go down there!" It can be frightening to stand at the top of the stairs looking down into the gloom and darkness because we're afraid of what's inside ourselves. It helps to enter these worlds with someone who's not afraid, someone who's been to the basement before and even goes there frequently—a skilled psychotherapist to lead the way.

Once we get there, what will we find? Memories, tears not shed, decisions made about how life works that need to be re-made, painful feelings we repressed, other people's pain, all things that Jung referred to as the Shadow.

To continue with this analogy, when the basement is clean, the whole house benefits. You are no longer afraid of what's inside or have to avoid going there. Often, the result of this inner housecleaning is a freeing up of energy that was previously used to ignore the work that needed to be done. So turning on the light in the basement, while not necessarily pleasant at first sight, is a freeing endeavor.

People often ask how long it takes to get a nice clean basement. No one can say for sure, but most probably longer than you would like. Then again, if you don't get started, it will never get done.

Don't Believe What You Think

There are many reasons we practice meditation. One of the most widely touted is its ability to help us manage stress and feel relaxed. This is all well and good; however, I think the most important benefit is that it teaches us to break our identification with our minds. We watch; we breathe; we observe our thoughts float by like clouds. When a particular thought captures our attention, we calmly notice and let it go.

Many if not most people are continually tortured by a steady stream of thoughts letting them know they don't measure up: not attractive enough, not lovable enough, not rich, and on and on. Actually, our culture encourages this, because when people are happy with themselves, they won't buy much, so better to have us worried that we smell bad, could use some products or services to look younger (as if looking our age is a bad thing), and keeping up on the latest trends.

These punishing thoughts have their origins in our childhoods as well as in the culture. Our parents may have been well-meaning, yet they instilled in us beliefs that we are not okay as we are, or that there is something wrong with our natural human urges and desires. Some of our parents were not particularly well-meaning, and in response to their cruelty, we made decisions that affect us today in negative ways.

171

Children who were treated unkindly often bring to adulthood unhelpful beliefs such as that they are fatally flawed, that love is not due to them, that love is painful and abusive. These ideas are learned from poor parenting; they are not inherent in themselves.

Part of the process of overcoming personal pain and suffering is to learn to stop believing every thought that you think. It is time to put to use the techniques you have learned while meditating. We cultivate an attitude of being the witness to our thoughts, rather than being identified with them. When we notice our unhelpful beliefs, such as "I'm no good," or "No one loves me," we gently notice that this is just the mind doing its thing, breathe, and let go.

The mind is designed to be useful as a problem solver, not to run our lives. The mind is very good with challenges such as how to build a bridge, or how to double a cookie recipe. It is not good at love or happiness or meaning. It can assist us with those pursuits, but is limited in its ability. You, not your mind, are meant to be in the driver's seat of your life. Your mind is a helpful tool when you learn how to use it by not believing everything you think.

Not Afraid of Anything Inside

"You're still angry with your father," I say.

"I don't think that will ever go away."

"It has to, if you want to become free."

Many people are afraid of what's inside them. They're afraid of silence, of being alone. Afraid of an unscheduled moment with nothing to do. If it gets too quiet, they're stuck with the contents of their own minds. Mostly, even though they don't consciously know it, they're afraid of the buried feelings inside they have never dealt with.

When you have hidden stuff inside such as still being angry with your father, it may surface when something occurs that is reminiscent of the original trauma, such as arguing with your lover. You find yourself responding in a much bigger way than the current situation warrants, because you are reacting to historical injury rather than to what's happening in the present.

One of the goals of psychotherapy is to clear all unresolved trauma out of the mind and body (although mainstream psychology does not know about this goal or possibility). In sessions, we work to clear thoughts, beliefs, energy patterns in the body, breathing, blockages and stuck places by the use of empathy, witnessing and being witnessed, counseling techniques, and by the client being in the presence of someone who has cleared her past and the inner silence that ensues.

Once you know it's possible to not be afraid of anything inside of you any more, wouldn't you want the freedom it offers? Imagine the places inside where you are no longer afraid to go, the conversations you'll no longer be anxious to have. A great deal of self confidence comes from knowing there's no longer anything shocking, shameful, horrible, or embarrassing to discover inside—it's all been dealt with.

Working through your hidden feelings is a significant investment of time and money. It's a tough road, but worth every bit of effort. Ignoring hidden feelings won't work, thinking positively won't do it, pretending it's not there, nor just talking or thinking about them without actually clearing the feelings out of your mind, body and energy field. Resisting the work is how many addictive behaviors are born.

Once you are free and clear, life will still bring challenges, but you will be able to handle them in the present rather than from a place entangled in the past. How long will it take? That depends on how difficult your early years were and how dedicated you are to resolution. You can make it, though. It is possible to not be afraid of anything inside any more.

The Great Art of Doing Nothing

Tiffany is looking at me as if I've lost my mind. She is a corporate executive for an international, brand-name company; a new mother, a sister, a friend, a daughter and a wife. She struggles to control her diet and stay fit. She wants to accomplish more with her time, not less. "Do nothing?" she asks plaintively. "And do what?"

Nothing's wrong with accomplishing a lot, as Tiffany does. Western culture is focused on achievement which requires a lot of "doing." People are asking more of their lives than ever before—we want to be successful financially, and have perfect health and great relationships. These are laudable aspirations, but we're out of balance, at the expense of non-doing or just "being." We've lost the great art of doing nothing at all.

I knew nothing about this until I spent a year at an ashram in India. It took awhile to wind down from my manic Western pace, but after I did, I fit in quite well. There was plenty of time to sit by the river, watch the clouds and cows grazing, meditate, enjoy leisurely meals, and spend lazy afternoons chatting with friends. Life was relaxed; we thought we were getting a lot accomplished if we mailed a letter that day.

Of course, the realities of needing to earn a living in-

175

truded, and it was time to go back to work. Too much leisure is deadening to the spirit which wants to be of service to its fellow beings. But I learned the great value of doing nothing at all, sometimes referred to as meditation. Some meditations suggest watching the breath or the thoughts; some concentrate on a mantra or sound. Some listen, which was especially delightful in the tropics, with the sounds of birds and roosters reminding us to wake up. All meditation methods involve doing nothing productive. They teach us to just "be."

One way to incorporate doing nothing into a busy life is to take up a meditation practice. A few minutes of quiet inwardness can balance many hours of outward doing-ness. However, I am reticent to prescribe meditation to my patients, as it often becomes one more item on the dreaded to-do list. It's often easier to do nothing whenever you can find a moment, such as in the car when you get home before going into the house.

The point isn't to live a life of non-doing. Instead, we can incorporate doing nothing into our lives in precious bits of time. We have to give up chastising ourselves for taking that time. We need to question our high standards for productivity. If we don't, we're in danger of losing the connection to that which makes life most meaningful.

Six Amazing Transformational Technologies That Are Absolutely Free

A lot of people call me who can't afford to pay for therapy. It's true that many of the most powerful ways to work on yourself cost a lot of money. Psychotherapy, high priced seminars, bodywork, yoga classes, nutritional supplements, and seeking advanced training in your field will all improve your life but take significant financial commitment. I personally don't regret a dollar of the many thousands I've spent on the above, but some people are reticent to make such an investment in themselves. Then again, some of the most effective technologies for change cost no money:

1) **Exercise** It's been proven over and over again that nothing works better for treating depression. Getting those endorphins pumped up raises your mood, not to mention how much better you look and sexier you feel. Here's a free program for how to Begin a Running Program from Scratch: http://www.marathontraining. com/faq/faq_br.html. I've used this twice myself, once to get started, and once again after a skating accident.

2) **12-Step Programs** They're not just for alcoholics anymore. You may be familiar with AA and the groups having to do with drug addiction, but are you aware of Debtor's Anonymous, which is highly effective

177

at teaching you how to get out of debt and handle your finances, or the relationship-help programs like Alanon and Sex and Love Addicts Anonymous (SLAA). Go online, find a meeting in your zip code, and check it out. It's shocking to meet all the people who are there just to help you for free.

3) **Clean Up Your Diet** You already know what you need to do. And no matter how well you eat, you can always do better. Start slowly or make a massive shift depending on what kind of results you want. Sugar, fat, fried foods, alcohol, coffee—in excess you know what they do to your body, but have you ever noted what they do to your moods?

4) **Take Time to Do Nothing** Some people call this meditation. Our culture is overly focused on productivity and success. See how restorative it is to be quiet, not to talk or read or listen to music or anything. My life changed radically when I learned to just BE instead of do, do, do.

5) **Complete Your Incompletes** Anything unfinished creates a drag on your energy. You can make measurable shifts in your life by finishing up loose ends: clean your house, get the recycling out, donate stuff you're not using anymore or sell it on *craigslist*. Get your life current and into integrity.

6) **Change the Focus of Your Attention** Concentrating on everything you imagine to be wrong with yourself and your world is a guaranteed prescription for feeling bad. Practice focusing on what's right, what's beautiful, and what's good.

These practices may not cost money, but they will require significant dedication in terms of time and intention. That in itself could be all the change you need.

There's an App for That

Give up your therapist? Not quite yet. But some exciting new trends in self help can be easily accessed right from your phone.

Most mobile phone apps are intended as an adjunct to therapy rather than a replacement for it. Patients can learn to relax themselves, monitor their moods, and attend 12-step meetings. Even the Veteran Affairs National Center has developed an app for those suffering from Post-traumatic Stress Disorder (PTSD Coach). Here are some possibilities:

- **Relaxation** Some of the most popular apps (iBreathe, Relax and Rest) are guided exercises leading the user into deeply relaxing states wherever one is, whenever needed.

- **Mood Journals** These apps (eCBTMood, Optimism) encourage people to graph their daily moods and develop strategies to manage them. Users are asked questions about their habits such as exercise, caffeine intake, and the prevalence of positive or negative self-talk. The user can learn to make different choices in the future as good preventive mental health care.

- **12-step Meetings** (Pocket Sponsor, iPromises) These apps help people recovering from addictions, offering affirmations, meditations, and support.

- **Dreams** Move aside, Dr. Freud. A new Japanese app ("Have a Good Dream") that is not yet available in English allows the user to control their dreams. The app tracks when users has entered REM sleep, then plays a soundtrack to encourage a dream state of their choice. Users are encouraged to interpret and share their dreams via social media.

- **Relationships** Need a Love Doctor? Leading relationship expert John Gottman, Ph.D., has developed an app (Love Apps) that asks pertinent questions to encourage closer sharing and intimacy.

- **Virtual Environments** The most exciting possibilities, however, are coming from the world of gaming. Developers are working on apps that will envelop the user in a fictional world wherein they will make choices that change the way they use their brains. An example would be an app for a socially anxious person who will enter an imaginary party and make confident choices that will provide a life-changing experience.

But change is not necessarily going to happen overnight. Research on the effectiveness of mental health apps is not conclusive. A recent study completed by Richard McNally, Ph.D., at Harvard proved that readers of the article about the research improved their scores on the test questionnaire in equal numbers to research participants. It seems we're all excited about the possibility of improving our life through apps, even if they don't work. Apps can't replace the warmth of human contact and caring that is present in a face-to-face therapy session. At least not yet.

Is Psychotherapy Out of Date?

He looked like Bradley Cooper but he didn't have a job. At cocktail parties, I'm used to receiving a showstopper response when I reply that my profession is "therapist" or "shrink," but this was a new one. "Psychotherapy," he said. "That was cool in the 80s, right?"

It's true that today's mainstream culture encourages shallow pursuits. Eighty-one percent of today's college students state that getting rich is their number one priority. The media attempts to continually brainwash us to believe that physical appearance, possessions, and leisure are the most important things in life. Yet there's also a 50-80 million person subculture evolving who state that their highest values include authenticity, helping others, being involved in creating a better way of life, and psychological and spiritual development. These longings may not be nurtured by the society at large, but they are timeless human ideals.

Certainly, there are types of therapy that are out of date. You don't see much demand for the nude encounter groups of the 80s any more (unfortunately?), or for meandering treatment that goes on for years and doesn't produce any tangible results. I believe that therapy will move to the phone and Skype as people choose to work with therapists who don't live in their

183

town, although many feel that the in-person connection is all important.

Some think that psychotherapy might be out of date because of the plethora of self-help information available on bookshelves and the Internet. All one needs to do is Google their symptoms to find advice on what to do. If that solves your problems, great—in fact, I often encourage people to do just that. Then again, this is often how people find out they can't do it by themselves. There is no replacement for building a relationship with someone who has had years of experience facilitating personal growth, who knows how the transformative process works, and who's been there herself.

What "Bradley" was talking about was that back in the 70s and 80s, the counter culture was very vocal about the benefits of working on oneself and experimented with various techniques to do so. Some of the charismatic therapists of the day achieved rock star status, and people were not shy about saying they were their patients. Today, as then, it actually is very "cool" when someone becomes free from parental and mainstream programming as a result of therapy, when they individuate into their own unique true self, because each person who becomes free helps the whole planet evolve. Getting help from a skilled psychotherapist to become your best self is actually more relevant today than it ever was.

How is Transpersonal Therapy Different from Mainstream Counseling?

People often ask me how transpersonal therapy differs from mainstream counseling. It differs in three major ways: how transpersonal therapists are trained, the context in which we hold therapy and, in some cases, the techniques we use or recommend to facilitate change.

Transpersonal therapists receive training in the same mainstream psychology as other therapists that is necessary to pass licensing exams. However, we are not satisfied with that as we don't believe the modern West has all the answers, so we acquire additional training in the psychologies of other cultures: Eastern religions, Native peoples, LSD research and other altered states of consciousness, mysticism, and the esoteric aspects of all religions, which Aldous Huxley dubbed "the perennial philosophy."

The context we offer is open to spirituality and alternate ways of knowing, making the space safe for people who identify as "spiritual," i.e. those for whom spiritual search is an integral and compelling part of their life. Spiritual people are often reluctant to enter mainstream therapy with good reason, as few conventional therapists know how to honor what is outside their own mindset. Spiritual people want to be able to talk with their therapists about their experiences with altered states of consciousness, their thirst for higher knowledge and abilities. They want to be understood for wanting to be free, truly free, even if it means challenging the status quo of the mainstream culture. They want help to untangle unhelpful patterns from the past the same as other clients, but they want it from people who have gotten free themselves.

The transpersonal context is one of support for alternate ways of knowing, of understanding that people may not want to adapt themselves to a culture that is itself sick, and that ours is not the highest state of evolution possible. It's understanding that sometimes the greatest things humans can know come from the heart rather than the mind, that compassion may be a greater value than consumerism, that striving to reach to one's potential is more fascinating than owning and wearing the right brands. The truly transpersonal embraces the brands, too, why not? But for people who have glimpsed a reality beyond that, it beckons and won't let them go. It becomes of utmost importance to remove the blocks that stand in the way of resting in the quiet space where lies the Truth of who we really are.

Techniques that transpersonal therapists utilize may include meditation, energy work, or other alternative modalities. The most important thing, however, is sound clinical skills, the ability to really "get" the client, and the therapist's commitment to their own ongoing growth.

The Blister and the Teakettle

People often ask what happens in psychotherapy. Sometimes, although more rarely than you might imagine, therapists give good old fashioned advice, and famously, we listen intently. Often, we teach skills that people missed in childhood, such as how to communicate or manage angry feelings. Therapy involves getting better in touch with your emotions or helping you to make healthier choices. This kind of assistance you can often get from a loving friend, self-help books, or the Internet.

Sometimes, though, what is needed is help to clean out old rubbish from the past, and this is deeper work you can't do with an untrained person. Osho, a spiritual teacher, once said that therapists are really people who help you take out your garbage.

One of the analogies I use to explain to patients what is going on is a blister. We've all had one: a pocket of fluid underneath the skin which has been caused by repetitive pressure or rubbing. The fluid inside is usually watery, but if it's been there for a long time untreated and become infected, it can be filled with pus or blood. To treat it, we carefully make a tiny puncture and drain the infected part, relieving the pressure and thereby allowing the healing process to begin.

This is an analogy for how material from the past—unexpressed emotions, outrage, sense of injustice, fear—can be trapped inside, while a protective covering has grown over to protect it. Therapy can be like this: We drain the old toxic material that has built up, thereby relieving the pressure and allowing the healing to begin.

The second analogy I use to explain the therapy process is a teakettle. You've seen one that is all hot and bothered, steam jetting out the sides. People with a lot of repressed material inside can get like this, spewing out all over the place. The "steam" tends to come out crooked, such as getting mad when you didn't mean to or acting in ways that surprise you, and not in a good way. The material leaks out from the inside because the pressure has built up too much and we need to work to relieve the pressure. In therapy we get the "heat" down to a normal level, so that we can sit and enjoy a cup of tea.

If you get with the right therapist and complete this work, you will agree that it was worth the commitment because of your new sense of freedom from the past. It is a joy to go through life without "blisters" or without the pressure of sitting on a hot stove.

Notes On Art as Therapy

1) At the end of his life, Timothy Leary apologized for having written so many books. The book, he said, is out of date, old technology, and therefore only adds to the pollution of the world.

2) "Writing as a Spiritual Practice" was the name of a workshop I once attended. The leader was a Zen nun with a severe grey crewcut and three-hour-a-day habit which she executed whether she felt like it or not, unlike me. When you write about painful material from the past, she taught us, the psychological issue will be fully resolved when the piece is complete.

3) "The transformation of waste is perhaps the oldest preoccupation of man," Patti Smith rants on *Easter*.

4) Another seminar I attended, this one called "River Stories," co-led by Kirsten Linklater, originator of the famed voice method, and Carol Gilligan, the distinguished Harvard psychologist, was attended by forty female actors and me. As one of the exercises, we wrote a song, a poem, a dialog, and a scene for four poignant moments of our lives. After I performed for the group my vignettes that had been transformed into "art," I felt better about my life than ever

189

before. By that time I'd acquired a long resume I could've been proud of, but it meant nothing to me because I'd never planned on a corporate career, nor did I value it. Creating stories, transforming the garbage into something worth sharing: I acknowledged for the first time the bravery of one little life.

5) "I don't know why to finish my book," I struggled. "Metaphysically, it makes no difference whether I finish it or not." Andy Couturier, writing midwife and decent person *extraordinaire*, raised his hands to his heart in the namaste gesture, then widened his arms, palms up, out into the world, bringing tears to my eyes.

6) After eight years, I've finished my book. I apologize in advance if it adds to the pollution of the world. Personally, I found that working with life events and turning them into fiction, fiction with its arc and mythic aspiration, liberated me from the quiet cell where emotions had entrapped me for years. When the book was finished, I could move on, and not a day before. Suddenly, the past no longer owned the best days of my life; now it was now; the best days are the present. Freedom, it spelled freedom. So I have learned: Do your art; create your thing; write your book. It's some of the best therapy in the world. Then, widen your arms and let it spread out, offering a tear to the worldwide heart.

You Might Prefer an Active Meditation

When most people hear the word "meditation," they envision a serenely calm person sitting blissfully, probably with their legs crossed in the lotus position. What is going on inside that meditator's head, however, may be a different story. Their mind is most likely struggling and overwhelmed with its many dramas, anxieties, and infatuations. Many people can't stick with a meditation practice because it is just too darn uncomfortable.

The benefits of meditation have been well documented: reduced stress, better health, concentration, spontaneity and creativity. There are purported psychological and spiritual benefits, such as helping to keep things in perspective, developing intuition, greater tolerance of others and self, and even enlightenment. Nearly everybody who learns about it agrees that meditation is a good thing.

Then why do so few practice it? Certainly the modern lifestyle of constant activity does not value sitting silently doing nothing. And it is difficult for us to drop into silence with so much on our minds.

Osho, the great spiritual teacher, invented active meditations because he said people today are different than they were when meditation was invented. Never before were people so identified with their minds as we are today. For modern people, it is necessary to first energize the body, then throw off accumulated thoughts and emotions before one can benefit from silence. Once this is done, silence comes on its own without struggle.

The most famous Osho meditations are Dynamic and Kundalini. Dynamic begins with a chaotic breath technique, followed by catharsis—throwing off repressed feelings and emotions. If you practice with others, you may see someone crying or calling out to their mother, and another person celebrating the release of repressed joy. (This person might even be you.) Following this is a Sufi technique, silence, and finally a brief dance of celebration and joy, welcoming the day. Silence has come on its own, not by being forced or endured.

Kundalini Meditation begins with shaking the pelvis, which most Westerners hold tensely, thus stopping its natural energy flow. Dancing and celebration follow, then the delicious utter relaxation and silence. Margot Anand, the famous tantra teacher, once said that if a woman has problems achieving orgasm, if she does Kundalini Meditation for a month, she will become able to surrender.

Osho invented many other popular meditations, such as Nadabrahma, No Mind, Chakra Sounds, Gourishankar, and my favorite, Natararaj. All that is important is to choose one and try it out for yourself. Bliss awaits.

Your Reward: A Bigger Problem

You've seen the *Corona* commercials portraying the idyllic life: leisurely lounging by the ocean, taking it easy with only a bathing suit and flip flops between you and the summer breeze. No work, no problems—the recipe for bliss.

Except in real life, it doesn't work that way. Most people who have a chance to live out this fantasy are surprised that it turns out to be a nightmare. After the first few hours, or days, they find themselves bored out of their skulls.

That's because human beings are problem-solving machines. We are meant to be continually creative, solving the problems of life. And when we find a solution to a problem, rather than graduating to some fantasy tropical problem-free zone, we graduate to having more interesting, complex problems to solve. As Buckminster Fuller said, "The reward of solving a problem is a bigger problem."

For example, Rob worked hard and mastered his job, so after two years he was promoted to a management position with a whole new set of interesting challenges, global in scope. Kim finally figured out a day job that was minimally demanding and paid well enough, so now she can use more of her time and energy to create her art.

193

Our reward for solving problems is not withdrawal into an aimless existence. People who do so often become depressed, energy-less, ill, or preoccupied with weird things. In my practice, I've noticed intelligent women with eating disorders who, as soon as they have a more interesting problem to solve, such as landing an absorbing job or deciding to mentor a child, forget all about their eating disorder. It has been replaced by a more interesting, higher-level problem.

Sometimes what appears to be depression is the existential boredom of a person who is not engaged with interesting problems. There is nothing creative going on. This is not to discount the multitude of other depressed people who have chemical imbalances in their brains, or are down due to life circumstances or childhood trauma, but this is one question to ask oneself.

Is your issue that you don't have interesting enough problems to solve? Pick a "problem" that is big enough to not bore you—add your life to the efforts to stop world hunger, or finally get started on that massive Great American Novel. Get engaged in solving a problem so interesting that you can never solve it in this lifetime. You'll find your passion for life kicks into gear.

Chapter 7

Evolutionary Consciousness

The Roots of Tantra, Part One

When you trace it all back there are only two paths, tantra and yoga. All traditions stem from one or the other root. The paths stemming from yoga are those that teach there is something to do to arrive at ultimate fulfillment. The seeker needs to learn to restrain the passions, discipline the body and the breath, and refrain from indulging in pleasures, including sex. One must mold and sculpt oneself into something worthy of God in order to progress along the spiritual path. This mindset becomes apparent in the whole Western ethos of striving, making, doing, or trying to get somewhere, anywhere or anyone other than who or where you are.

Tantra, on the other hand, is the path that teaches that all is divine. In yoga, some things are holy and some things are not. In tantra, everything is perfect just the way it is, including darkness, death, difficult emotions, and sensual pleasures. No matter what is happening, it is celebrated as part of precious Life. The path to ultimate realization is in the full acceptance of the perfection of the present moment. There is nowhere to go; nothing to do, no one to be; all is as it is, and realizing this, one can surrender into a deep let-go.

In its central worldview that all is divine, tantra accepted our sensual nature as an essential facet of being human.

Tantrikas would experiment with what was forbidden by other traditions such as eating meat, drinking wine, and having sex, as a way of experiencing that all is a manifestation of the Divine, that the distinctions taught by society are false. These activities were performed in special ceremonies as specific occult techniques, much like the homeopathic remedy of ingesting a tiny bit of the poison that caused the illness in order to cure it.

Of course, today when all is permitted in Western society, the performance of such 'forbidden' actions carries no meaning. Eating meat and drinking alcohol are activities that no longer teach us anything and have, in fact, become stale. Instead, many people's lives have led to a sickening over-satiation of sensual pleasure, causing obesity, degenerative disease, and rampant boredom. Having sex is no longer forbidden, and for many people has become one of the paths of learning. It was said that in the Kali Yuga, which is the name of the time we are living in, tantra would reappear to enlighten the public.

The Roots of Tantra, Part Two

Great psychologists such as Sigmund Freud and Wilhelm Reich pointed out that the majority of people are starved for sexual fulfillment causing all kinds of ills, such as child abuse, rape, frigidity, compulsive sexuality, and obsessions of all sorts. This starvation, however, is not from lack of opportunity as it was in the past. The modern world offers plenty of images of sexuality, plenty of messages that to be sexually active is to be healthy, but gives little information about the connection between love, spirituality, and sex. Pornography has replaced nourishing sharing. The worship of lust has overshadowed the esoteric purpose of sex, which is to heal, purify, and ultimately dissolve all into Love.

So on one hand, you have the yogic paths that condemn sex, and on the other the tantric which elevate it to the level of a sacrament. Both roads have their dangers. The probable pitfall of the yogic path is an enormous inflation of ego. The yogi identifies with all that has been accomplished. The tantric path was forbidden because the danger is that one will become enthralled and addicted to the sensual circus. The pitfall with tantra is the fall into dissolution from which one may never emerge. Many paths today attempt to be a combination of the two. You will notice some tantric schools that are billed as "the yoga of sex." These approaches are arduous and involve much training of the body and breath.

When sex is allowed and encouraged, one will eventually come to the point where they discover that the fulfillment one is seeking from sex is not to be found in sex. The search for Union with the Beloved can only be realized through union with the universal, not with another person, and not through the body. The body and the beloved can offer glimpses, but not the ultimate. That is for what we search. Sex leads to what we are seeking only in the transcendence of it. When one is complete, sex disappears on its own.

In tantra, we go deeply into sex in order to complete it. When there is no repression left, no desire because it has been seen through, no more interest, we see that there is nothing there. We go Beyond. We become Complete. Those of us on the tantric path prefer to go through sex to get there, that's all. The purpose of tantra is to go beyond sex, but it seems difficult to interest anyone in this aspect of it. Most people would prefer not to develop to the point of transcending sex in this lifetime.

The Sacred Prostitute in the Ancient World

It may be hard for the Western mind to reconcile that the words sacred and prostitute may be linked, for the Judeo-Christian tradition holds sexuality to be profane, the antithesis of spirit. Yet in the times of the Great Goddess worship, sexuality was revered and held sacred. We find evidence of sacred prostitution throughout the ancient world, as early as the Gilgamesh Epic of 7000 B.C.E. Herodotus, a Greek historian from the third century B.C.E., wrote:

> *"...women of the land... sit in the temple of love and have intercourse with some stranger... the men pass and make their choice. It matters not what be the sum of money; the women will never refuse, for that were a sin, the money being by this act made sacred. After their intercourse she has made herself holy in the sight of the goddess..."[1]*

Sacred prostitution occurred in the early civilizations of Sumer, Babylonia, Egypt, Lebanon, and Rome, and is mentioned in the code of Hammurabi. It also seems to have been common in Europe and the Middle East prior to the rise of Judaism, Christianity, and Islam. In fact, sacred prostitutes not only existed, they flourished and were held to be important members of society:

> *"...the sacred prostitutes were many in number. According to Strabo, at the temples of Aphrodite in Eryx and Corinth there were above a thousand, while at each of the two Comanas about six thousand were in residence. They were accorded social status and were educated. In some cases, they remained politically and legally equal to men."* [2]

The Golden Age of goddess worship, in which sacred prostitution was widespread, was the Age of Taurus, whose polarity is Scorpio, the two signs most commonly associated with sexuality. Venus is the ruler of Taurus, and Venus as a goddess is physically beautiful and sexually appealing. She is the goddess of earthly love, sexual and sensual. The Great Goddess was the bringer of all that is alive, responsible for the fruitfulness of the earth. Through her came new life, and sexuality was one of the mysteries of creation. Sexuality was revered and worshiped in a way we find hard to fathom today. In the goddess temples, the sacred prostitutes were her priestesses. Their bodies were available to share the blessings of the goddess with strangers, hungry for love and connection. In this way, sexual love was shown to be divine, of the goddess, not separate from it. Hesiod, an eighth century B.C.E. poet, wrote:

> *"...the sensual magic of the sacred whores 'mellowed the behavior of men.' ...She is the bringer of sexual joy and the vessel by which the raw animal instincts are transformed into love and love-making."* [2]

These women were known in ancient languages as the *nu-gig*, or "the undefiled," "the pure or spotless."[3] This seems particularly to be of the nature of Virgo, that a woman known for her beauty and sexuality would be considered pure. The priestess felt herself to be an incarnation of the holy spirit as she made love with the men who came to pay homage to the goddess. She was a teacher of the mysteries, of the healing and restorative power of sexual energy.

1) M. Esther Harding, *Woman's Mysteries: Ancient and Modern*, New York, NY: Harper Colophon Books, 1971

2) Nancy Qualls-Corbett, *The Sacred Prostitute: Eternal Aspect of the Feminine*, Toronto, Canada: Inner City Books,1988

3) Ibid., pg. 34

Menopause Misunderstood

One of the best-kept secrets is how great menopause is. Women in the West are taught to fear The Change as the time when hair will grow on our chins, and even worse, we won't care. Men are taught to see menopause as gross and unspeakable. Both men and women are brainwashed to believe it's the death knell of a woman's attractiveness.

The time preceding menopause, called perimenopause, is certainly far from great. Mood swings, anger out of nowhere, hot flashes, night sweats, sleep problems and the fact that desire becomes erratic or completely evaporates can be hard to take. As are the sudden disappearance of portrayals of any women your own age in the media, and the fact that the checkers at Trader Joe's start calling you "ma'am."

The word "menopause" actually means when a woman hasn't had a menstrual period for a year, so these symptoms will have subsided into a calm state of well being, never again to be plagued by PMS.

There is little to no guidance in the mainstream culture about the true nature of menopause. Western medicine considers it a disease to be treated, and youth culture scorns any signs of aging. We are being sold a bill of goods, so we turn against ourselves. Women in their 40s and 50s are the highest age group on antidepressants.

However, if you look deeper, you will find Gail Sheehy who wrote *A Silent Passage*, first a bombshell article in *Vanity Fair* and a subsequent book, in which she provided research to show that women over 50 are in the most powerful time of their lives. All the energy not being used to raise kids can be directed to other pursuits, often toward the arts, the community, and in general, improving life around them.

According to Kevin Fortune, a sex educator from Northern California, during menopause the Kundalini energy is refiguring itself. Hot flashes are actually bursts of Kundalini energy opening a woman to her deeper spiritual wisdom. Kevin sees the transition of menopause as a "magical time" when "tremendous energy becomes available for spiritual transformation."

In sex-negative cultures, the only purpose of sex was procreation, so when a woman couldn't give birth any more, her "usefulness" was finished. Barbara Marx Hubbard, the famed futurist, writes that there is an evolutionary purpose for the fact that there are more postmenopausal women alive on the planet today than have ever existed. She states that the freed-up energies of postmenopausal women are going to save the world, and has renamed it "regeneropause."

Rather than buy into the prevalent myth that menopause is a time of decline, women can be guided to the fact that menopause is a time of profound change which allows us to expand into our power and creativity. It is a gateway to a deeper connection with our spirituality and purpose.

One Humiliating Thing
After Another

Tracy secretly felt better than everyone at the networking group. The others were not as polished as she or as well dressed and were quite a bit older. Later, when she found out the entire group was composed of successful business owners, while she herself had been unable to get her own business off the ground, she felt shamefully embarrassed that she had been so quick to judge.

In therapy, David came to realize the part he's played in his relationship failures. This painfully didn't align with his previous belief that the women in his life had been at fault. Claire became aware that the joke she'd played had really been an attack as it cost her one of her best friends.

In my experience, the spiritual path is a long chain of one such humiliating realization after another. I've never heard anyone say this, but as I've shared this observation with others, it seems to be distressingly common. What you thought you were, you are not. Every fantasy you had about yourself gets busted. You have not been particularly loving. You are not as great or as important as you imagined. Other people could, for the most part, not give a fig about what you eat, what you are wearing, whether or not you are a good dancer.

Everything you were clinging to about your identity is

challenged. Over time, you realize how unloving you've been, how arrogant, and how much smaller than you dreamed. You're never going to be a celebrity, rich, loved by all, or as successful as you wanted to be.

Our culture promotes narcissism, competitiveness, surface over depth. Even our spirituality is often superficial: We take pride in attending the hippest yoga class taught by the most prestigious teacher; in how our bodies look, in how superior our path, and in how cleanly we eat. Spiritual people are often competitive over which whole food products they buy and whether they and others are up on the latest food fad—coconut water, coconut oil, raw foods, green drinks.

When we suffer the true humiliation that comes from seeing our arrogance, it is life changing. We become right-sized, not seeing ourselves as too big, which is inflated, or too small, which is groveling. When we feel the sting of realization that we have hurt people with our casual rejection, our superficial judgments or our lack of love, our hearts can break, and we can share ourselves more readily. We can confront our narcissism and our enormous selfishness. That is truly progress on the spiritual path.

Ego Backlash

Annie hadn't known it could get this good. Over the weekend, she'd surrendered to the love flowing for herself and everyone else. The workshop had provided a safe environment for participants to let down their guards, their judgments and insecurities and simply be as they are. Annie allowed herself to feel vulnerable, and people responded with love and affection. She opened up to a whole new level of trust in Existence.

So it came as a big surprise when the letdown followed. Annie found herself quite discouraged. Nothing at the workshop seemed real now that she was back facing her same old unsatisfying life. Nothing seemed worth it, all this working on herself. Her faults came into sharp focus. The disappointment was as overwhelming as the previous experience was high.

What Annie is experiencing is called ego backlash. It's similar but not the same as the inevitable low that follows every high, such as the hangover after enjoying drinking, the Monday morning after a vacation, or coming down from psychedelic drugs. Ego backlash is the low that follows a particularly expansive, heart-opening experience.

When you taste freedom from the individual self, the ego becomes frightened. It knows that if you become free, it won't be in charge any more so it fights for its life, sometimes viciously. If you become a person full of love, the ego's existence is threatened. It will no longer be in control, so it doubles its efforts to keep you trapped and afraid of your freedom. The ego's job is to keep you small and frightened. That's the game. It's not malevolent; it's trying to keep you safe.

Every time you have a significant growth experience, your ego will provide you with a backlash. Once you learn that this is predictable, you can prepare for it. You can realize that it will rear its head and not take it so seriously. You can listen to the mental criticism and "helpful hints" to see if there is something valid about the thoughts or you can turn the sound off all together. You can be matter-of-fact about knowing ego backlash is an inevitable part of the process of spiritual growth.

You've probably heard the adage about personal growth that it's "two steps forward and one step back." The step backward is inevitable, but it doesn't negate that you are still a step ahead. And when you take the next two steps forward, you will be that much further on your way toward personal and spiritual freedom.

Let Go

One of the most formative moments in my life was in a tantra group in India when our teacher, Radha Luglio, was asked how to open more: to more love, more sexual pleasure, more life. Her answer still rings in me: "I don't try to open more, instead, I become aware of where I am closed."

This is completely opposed to how we conceive of things in the West. If something is broken, we want to fix it. If there is something we can't do, we want to become able to do it. If we can't speak Spanish, we will take Spanish lessons. We will hire a personal trainer because we want to acquire a certain type of body. If we want love, we will read books to acquire knowledge about how to get it or take classes or seminars. We try to force the opening.

But what Radha and the tantra perspective are offering is that all this forcing of the acquisition of skills and knowledge is not necessarily the way. We only need relax and become aware of what is happening in the moment. It is not that there is no love; it is that we are guarded against it. It is not that we need to do something for greater sexual pleasure; it is that it is helpful to notice how we are defended against it. More life equals more openness to how things are, not more forcing of how we want things to be.

When I offer this perspective to clients and ask them to notice where they are holding, they are always able to locate it. I have never met a client who cannot easily notice where in their body it resides. The holding is not usually in our conscious awareness, rather just below the surface.

When we notice where we are holding, we take responsibility for our condition instead of blaming outside factors or other people for why we don't have more love or sex in our lives. We can take up disciplines such as meditation and bodywork to help us relax into a state of "let go" in our bodies and our lives.

So, right now, notice where you're holding any tension. Maybe in your shoulders, your neck, your pelvis. You might take a breath and see if it loosens a little, but if it doesn't, just notice that, too. No need to do anything. Just breathe and become more aware of yourself and the human condition. We are all like this, afraid of more love, more "let go," more surrender—the very things we want the most.

Pet Therapy

Witches have black cats. Dogs are "man's best friend." Hamsters and gerbils are cute as they can be, and some people even like snakes.

I picked Frankie the cat up from the shelter last week and carried her to her new home. She immediately ran for cover under the bed and wouldn't come out for 24 hours. When she began tentatively venturing out, she would run back whenever she got spooked, often just because someone was walking by, leading to the conclusion she might have been previously abused. A couple of times now she has let me stroke her and scratch her head, and then I get my reward: the magic motor of her purring starts and doesn't stop, that is, until she runs back under the bed again. Thank god, she came knowing how to use the cat box.

I just found out on the Internet that back in the Middle Ages during the holocaust of women and gays they designated "witches," they also perpetrated a huge massacre of cats. The Church was afraid of these "familiars" of the so-called witches because it was believed that cats had psychic powers and could help perform spells. There was even a dog that was tried and hanged as a witch in the Salem witch trials. When you look deeply into Frankie's mysterious blue eyes, you can almost believe they were right—she knows something we don't.

Pets seem to have been put into our lives for one purpose and one purpose only: to love and be loved. There's plenty of well-documented research that being around animals reduces people's stress levels, lowers blood pressure and even helps us live longer. Animal assisted therapy has been used with at-risk teenagers, folks in nursing homes, AIDS patients, and heart attack victims. I got a call recently from a prospective patient who wanted to know if I had a "therapy dog," which was the first time I'd heard the term (and no, I don't, although I'm thinking about training Frankie). On a brochure for an expensive recovery center I got in the mail, they list "equine therapy" as a treatment modality, which really means it makes people feel better to ride a horse.

I guess the gist of this is that lonely people everywhere could benefit from owning a pet. There's something about that unconditional love that's harder to get from flawed human beings. Also, here in LA, it's a way that people shop for lovers—going to the dog park to meet other dog owners. It's easy to talk to someone with a dog, right? No ulterior motive other than just being friendly. Guess we'll need to get them to set up cat and gerbil parks for everyone else.

Giving More Than You Get

Back in the 90s, I studied with Robert Kiyosaki, the multi-millionaire author of the *Rich Dad* series of financial advice books. He was "only" worth four million at the time, years before he became much richer and world famous. Robert taught us that the number one thing he attributed his success to was tithing, the practice of giving away ten percent of your money. Even when his business tanked and he and his wife were starting over with nothing, they tithed, giving away the first ten percent of their income.

Around the same time, I had a problem with keeping a job, and when I realized it, became desperate to heal my pattern. The next time I was hired I worked really hard, harder than ever before by a long shot. I wasn't making much money but instead of focusing on it, I decided they couldn't fire me if I produced more for them than they were paying me for. Not only did I keep my job but that attitude got me promoted twice.

When you set out to give more than you receive, whether in money or time, it comes back. Without getting too "woo woo" here, giving comes first, before receiving and not the other way around.

Robert taught us to pay our tithe to organizations that

inspire us. There's a long-standing tradition to tithe to one's church or religious organization, and if that's your thing, great. Personally, I'm moved by how Doctors Without Borders provides free medical care around the world with no regard to war or politics. I'm sure you have your favorites among the nonprofits working for the common good. The point is that you give to groups who are doing positive work for people and the planet before you give to yourself.

There's also an additional psychological benefit: Giving this way busts the old conditioning that money is evil, and that you'll be a bad person if you have money. It's impossible to hold those ideas if you're consistently giving away money and supporting the good. It sets up an attitude of abundance when you see the organizations you are supporting working effectively to bring about change.

I've never done tithing perfectly or fully at the suggested ten percent. But I do notice that the more I give, the more magic happens in my life. Begin today, being generous and attempting to give more than you receive. You'll find it impossible, but it's a fun game.

It's Not Enough to Evolve Yourself

The self-improvement business is booming. Videos, books, classes, teleseminars, newsletters, gyms, get-away weekends: The opportunities to improve yourself are endless. Whether it's diet, fitness, attractiveness, ability to make money, relationships, or sexual skills, there is a myriad of offerings at all price points.

People are caught up in the self-improvement business, but nobody seems to ask what are we improving ourselves for? The promise is more happiness, and to a certain extent, becoming healthy, affluent, and more able to have better relationships will make you happier.

But after we are healthy enough, affluent enough, and have decent relationships, the danger is that all this continuing work on ourselves serves to increase our egotism. People are secretly working hard to prove they are better than other people. A hotter body, a purer diet, more money and a better lover—many people appear to be trying to achieve superman status, a superman/woman who towers above mere mortals.

None of these aspirations for health, wealth, and relationships is bad in and of itself. Developing skills is helpful and right, but after that, what? Seems to me, if it's not to become more loving, then it's all narcissism.

A healthy body is essential so that we can work and love better. More money is necessary so we can meet our own needs first, then figure out how to help others, either by tithing or by developing goods and services to contribute to making the world a better place.

The purpose of becoming a better lover is not for self-aggrandizement but to make more love. Timothy Leary explains that at one evolutionary stage one acquires tantric skills to have them, which then leads to the next stage wherein one achieves fusion with a partner. Together, you create a level beyond which neither of you could go by yourself.

Maybe it's best to say that we need to evolve to a certain point and after that, further attention to ourselves becomes narcissistic. The next evolutionary stage after "enough" is to turn one's attention to what one can do for others with all the available knowledge, skill, wealth, wisdom, improved mood, healthy and fit body.

So, it's not enough to evolve yourself; it has to be for others. You become a better person so you can contribute to the ongoing evolution of others. That is the meaning of the concept of the *bodhisattva*, a graceful being who focuses on the evolution of others rather than only on what serves herself.

The Geography of Holiness

We had ridden on the motorbike an hour to get there, to the little room inside a cave in India, far off the tourist track. When Peter opened the door, it was to freezing cold air, water dripping into a tiny pond, and the tinny sounds of a cassette tape of prayers sung in Sanskrit on continuous loop. The spirit of holiness was palpable, thick from years of chanting, decades—who knows how long—in India it might be millennium. The energy quieted the mind of its chatter and still resonates in my consciousness today.

Some places carry the energy of the Divine. We might feel this when entering an ancient cathedral or shrine. The New Age has identified global places of power such as Machu Picchu, Lourdes, Sedona, and the Amazon jungle. Perhaps you have felt the opposite of this feeling in parts of the inner city where crimes are committed daily.

From the Buddhists comes the concept of the *buddha-field*, the environment that blossoms around a person of high spiritual attainment. The geographical area becomes purified by the compassionate actions of the Enlightened One, and thus is conducive to spiritual practice and advancement. The buildings and pathways in these *buddhafields* are often built of marble, believed to store the Enlightened One's energy for two thousand years.

Certain places are reported to consist of the sanctified energy of people praying and meditating there for centuries. This also has to do with the saying of Jesus, "Wherever two or more are gathered in my name, I am there among them." Wherever people gather to worship, work on themselves, be of service, seek Truth; wherever like-minded people gather with other seekers, the power of the group raises everyone.

Also from the Buddhists comes the precept of devotion to the *sangha*, the community of spiritual seekers. All the meditation, prayer, commitment to an art or craft, support and love enhance everyone participating in it. You will be able to identify a *buddhafield* or a *sangha* because around this vibration, your mind will become quiet, your body relaxed, and your energy will rise to meet it. You will feel a deep understanding that all is as it is.

What does this mean to we urban dwellers who may not live in a *buddhafield* and may, in fact, live in the inner city? That we may benefit from paying closer attention to our environment and our group of friends. We may need to spend time searching for our *sangha*, or spiritual brothers and sisters. We can choose to visit *buddhafields* when on vacation, or create them in our apartments and communities. Together, we can work to create energy fields that lift us all up.

It's Not Supposed to Last

The allure of a permanent state of happiness—imagining the possibility is an essential part of being human. We dream that if we do the right things or have it all, we'll achieve the pain-free, permanently happy life that we imagine celebrities or the super rich have. Advertising promotes the fantasy that happiness can be purchased as possessions, leisure, status, and lifestyle, all of which may contribute to happiness, certainly, but there are no guarantees.

Notice that as soon as you download a new song from *iTunes*, you're tired of it. The dessert you carefully chose from the menu never tastes as good as you'd hoped, and when you try to repeat a pleasure that at one time made you ecstatic, it's always disappointing. Our frustration prompts us to try to repeat an experience that one time brought us pleasure, as we become dulled against the truth that it can't be done. We try to shift our moods by taking a pill, drinking alcohol, bingeing on food, or watching porn, all activities famous for facilitating momentary happiness, but, in the long run, they may create deep rooted and difficult-to-eradicate addictions.

Many of my patients express that, "all I want is to be happy," by which they mean constantly positive and joyful, never negative, sad, depressed, or feeling angry or grief-stricken. Some people have even gotten to the point that if they aren't happy all the time, they blame themselves and believe there's something wrong with them. This frustration comes from a misunderstanding regarding the nature of happiness—it's not supposed to last.

It's not supposed to last so that you will go on searching for something that does last. You are supposed to be continually frustrated in your search. The fact that happiness is transient is necessary to lead you to that which will make you truly fulfilled, rather than momentarily elated. True happiness cannot be found in that which is impermanent.

Certainly, there are many things you can do and ways to live your life that will make you happier, such as manage your finances, get enough exercise, and live according to your moral code. But no matter what you do, a permanent state of happiness will elude you until you find it in something other than that which doesn't last. It is possible to develop a sense of happiness about whatever is happening, a sense of celebrating all the flavors of life: sadness, lack, boredom, and even the fact that happiness is not supposed to last.

It's Not Supposed to Last, Part Two

When I lived in India for a year, meditating daily, surrounded by other seekers, and enjoying the relaxed ashram life, I entered a state of happiness I thought would never end. Finally, it seemed I had achieved what I had been reading about for years. It was ecstatic, every single day. I even planned to write a book when I got home: how to heal your depression for good.

Unfortunately, my happiness went away with a THUD when I got back to the West, bringing a depression that was as low as my previous state was high. My chronic depression was perhaps more virulent than ever, now that I was aware of what I had lost. My therapist at the time had never experienced what I had, but he was kind and solid as an oak. "I think your depression is the absence of That," he said.

I ran around looking for answers and found some when I was sitting in a small group of seekers surrounding Eli Jaxon-Bear. "I thought it would never go away," I cried when it was my turn to talk. Everyone in the group started chuckling softly. "You're chasing the high," Eli said. "Look at your pattern of addictions." I didn't think I still had them, but there they were—addictions to certain ways of thinking, to expectations, to ideas about how things should be—subtler than I had previously been able to detect.

These high states are not supposed to last. They are little tastes of the Ultimate—the carrot at the end of the stick. They are little morsels to keep us on track, to keep us searching for the real stuff.

People who have peak experiences, either through drugs, through meditation, through sex, or through Grace, often imagine that they have now arrived. It is beyond-belief painful when the realization sets in that the peak won't be permanent. However, it was predictable, because every high is followed by the low, every mountain has its valley; that is, until you reach the summit of Everest, or so I've been told.

After the taste, the work resumes: the work on oneself to become more aware, more kind, more surrendered. More open to life, to love, to the divine. Like anything else worth having in life, it takes a lot of work to get there. The little tastes of happiness that don't last can be reminders to not lose heart and to keep going until you're home.

Chapter 8

Finding Our Way Home

Four Ways Spirituality Can Hurt You

Don't get me wrong—spirituality is a good thing. In today's world, most people could benefit from becoming more in touch with their spirituality, not less. In my practice, however, I see ways that New Age spirituality is hurting people. Here are things to look out for:

1) **You believe that by thinking positively or by saying affirmations, life will follow your whims and dictates.**

   In psychology, we call this "magical thinking." In reality, it takes a lot of hard work to accomplish your dreams, to live the life to which you aspire. Thinking right is an important part of the process, but it is only the very beginning.

2) **You take the idea that "you create your own reality" a little too far.**

   I see people who are full of self-blame and loathing because they hate themselves for their childhoods or for the way their lives have turned out. This line of taking full responsibility can be helpful, but there are limits. A world outside of us exists. Many cancers are caused by toxins in the environment. The children in the Sudan who had their arms chopped off in the war weren't creating that reality for themselves—someone very cruel was forcing it on them.

3) You believe that the light can exist without the dark, or that the light is the only thing of value.

Many people are searching for a simple solution to become happy all the time, which can lead them to deny their more difficult feelings, such as grief or anger, thinking them to be "not spiritual." On the contrary, these more difficult feelings serve a purpose, often letting us know when we are off track, when we have hurt someone, or when a change in our behavior is needed. The attitude of discounting the dark can lead to addiction—always looking for a high.

4) You don't do your psychological work because you believe it will just go away if you're spiritual enough.

You believe that meditating more will cure your depression, or that doing more yoga will cure your relationship problems. You don't understand the difference between psychology and spirituality, or that freeing yourself of your personal blocks can actually accelerate your spiritual growth. There are therapists who specialize in psychotherapy for spiritual people as here at The Transpersonal Counseling Center. Getting the help you need from a psychotherapist who understands the special needs of the spiritual path can be a life-changing step on your personal journey.

A Strategy for Compassion

Back when I was studying for my NLP (NeuroLinguistic Programming) Certification, we were taught that if one person can do something well, anyone can figure out the strategy and replicate it themselves. NLP'ers were busy systematizing all kinds of strategies for excellence: better golf swings, improved eyesight, weight loss, and successful business applications. All fine and good, I thought, but why aren't we codifying something important, such as how to increase levels of compassion?

Buddhists offer a variety of techniques for increasing compassion: various mantras, meditations, remembrances, and so forth. I'm sure many people derive benefit from these practices. The problem is, it's preaching to the choir. Anyone who would spend time every day practicing techniques to increase compassion is probably already high on the scale of open heartedness.

It seems to me that the Universe itself contains an in-built strategy for increasing our compassion, whether we want it or not, and whether or not we recognize it as such. When we suffer, which is an inevitable part of the human condition, our hearts break, and in that breaking is the possibility of the growth of compassion. When we hear about the suffering of others—the birds damaged by the BP oil spill, the victims of

Hurricane Katrina or the earthquake in Haiti, the Tibetan nuns and monks tortured and murdered by the Chinese—the pain can seem unbearable. And then on a personal level, we all experience grief and loss, maybe when a love affair ends or through the death of a loved one. We feel overcome with pain because we don't want anything to end, including our own lives. No one on this planet escapes having their heart broken.

The message in America seems to be to avoid suffering at all costs—take a pill, drink alcohol, eat a bunch of carbs and zone out, watch TV—anything other than allowing this inherent process of compassion expansion to work its magic. When our main goal is to not feel bad, we miss this natural maturation process that teaches us to love and care for our fellow human beings.

When we learn to stop fighting the fact of suffering, we can accept it as a purposeful process in our lives. When we allow our hearts to break, we become more open and loving towards those close to us and to the whole world. Go ahead, experience the cracking of your own heart, then let it break open some more. Allow the walls that keep it small and selfish to expand until you include all and everything in your love.

How Working on Your Business
Is a Spiritual Path

People often consider their spiritual work to be a separate arena from their work life. In truth, the workplace can function as an ideal environment in which you get paid to grow spiritually. Here are six ways:

- **You have the opportunity to confront your grandiosity.**

  The daily tasks it takes to become successful in business confront the glamour, fame, and wealth the ego feels is its due. On the career path, you start at the bottom and work your way up. The ego humbles itself in the process of admitting how much you don't know.

- **You learn how to work.**

  To be successful at anything takes an inordinate amount of effort. Much of New Age thought has hurt its adherents, hypnotizing them into believing that all they have to do to "manifest" wealth and a life of their dreams is to think the right thoughts. To achieve anything on this plane of existence takes much effort and repeated actions toward a goal.

- **You learn to plant seeds and wait for the harvest.**

  A farmer sows more seeds than needed because she doesn't know which ones will sprout. Many of the ef-

231

forts you make to be successful at work will not produce results, now or ever, yet you must make them. We learn through our work life to take action consistently and wait patiently for the payoff.

- **You learn to be of service to something bigger than yourself.**

  In other words, you practice *karma yoga*, the yoga of selfless service. Children and narcissists are only interested in what serves themselves; mature human beings are interested in using their lives in service of something more, whether their families, the company they work for, their communities, or a Higher Power.

- **You earn real, lasting self esteem instead of the fake kind that comes from repeating affirmations.**

  "Self esteem comes from performing estimable acts." This slogan from 12-Step Programs teaches us that self esteem must be earned and does not come from living in a selfish way.

- **You reap the benefits of being engaged in Right Livelihood, one of the elements of Buddha's Noble Eightfold Path to awakening.**

  It feels good to know that your work helps create a better world. If your job is to sell cigarettes you might not enjoy that feeling, but all the butchers, bakers and candlestick makers, teachers, doctors and street cleaners are making significant contributions to the human adventure.

Spiritual Bypass: How Not Working on Your Stuff Can Stunt Your Spiritual Growth

Throughout yoga class, Jennifer feels fat. She's obsessed with the other women's bodies—how much thinner, more limber, and more beautiful they are. Afterwards, at Whole Foods she buys a package of Organic Fig Bars and a pint of Carob Almond Rice Dream, goes home, eats it all, and throws up. Self-hatred quickly follows.

Kyle is late with his rent again and can't be sure he's not overdrawn. It's always this chaos, every month. That reservation he made for the weeklong meditation retreat was more than he could afford—but maybe he'll get some answers there.

Jennifer and Kyle are examples of what we call spiritual bypass: when a person's spiritual intentions and aspirations are sincere, but their unfinished business is holding them back.

People become attracted to spirituality in the hope it will solve life's problems and relieve pain and suffering, but it's not quite that simple. A popular misconception is that spiritual practice will in and of itself resolve psychological issues. Bestselling books advocate that by ignoring our discomfort and focusing on the Light, or on what we wish to manifest, we can get everything we want. This idea of positive thinking, or the law of attraction, can divert us from our real issues.

You can't make progress on the spiritual path if you're ignoring your pain. Pain, in fact, is an indication of where you need to grow—by pretending we're happy all the time, we miss the lessons our suffering and humanity are trying to teach us. As Alan Cohen says in *Wisdom of The Heart*, "If you desire to know where your spiritual work lies, look to your emotional pain."

When we have unmet needs, they will clamor for our attention and divert us from our path. Hence, we end up battling addictions, psychological issues, and not living our right life, rather than making the spiritual progress we hoped. Failing to discriminate between pseudo-spirituality and true inner transformation, we can get lost for years or life times.

Kyle and Jennifer and others like them are sincere spiritual seekers, but not dealing with their psychological issues is stunting their spiritual growth. Jen needs to get help from an eating disorder therapist, or depending on the severity of her problem, spend some time in a treatment program. Kyle needs to understand that being on a spiritual path doesn't negate needing to learn how to handle money. Working with a psychotherapist who specializes in understanding the pitfalls of the spiritual path could make all the difference in the world.

Spiritual Search Is the Reward of Prosperity

If we understand Maslow rightly, once one's basic needs are met, we are free to move up the pyramid to explore our higher level needs. Once we no longer have to worry about food and shelter, like folks in the prosperous West, we can devote our time to our needs for Love and Belonging, Esteem, and Self Actualization. We can graduate from concerns about finding a job that will pay for the basic necessities, for example, to finding the right job that will help us fulfill our creativity and own special gifts.

The human need for Love and Belonging is for friends, a lover, a family, and to be a vital member of the community. If you feel isolated and unloved, the pain will cause one to be stuck in their personal development until these needs are met. I often think of how primitive humans existed in small tribes; we haven't evolved out of this need for being part of a small group. In our lonely cities, many are struggling to feel connected, and new communities are springing up online.

Esteem needs are the next level of Maslow's pyramid, which means needing respect from others, a certain degree of status, self-confidence, achievement, independence, self-respect. The word on the street is that this should all come from within, but it's a human need to want to be acknowledged by one's community.

The top level is Self Actualization which Maslow said only 2% of people achieve. Here, an individual enjoys the desire to fulfill their potentials, to be all that one can be, to become one's most complete, fulfilled self. These people tend to enjoy solving problems rather than finding them burdensome, have a great degree of acceptance of self and others, and tend to have increased spontaneity, nonconformity, and creativity.

Self Actualize-ers also tend to have what are called Peak Experiences, or moments that make you feel One with God or nature. There is a feeling of being part of the Infinite and Eternal, and people having this experience report being changed forever for the better. Sometimes these peaks are called mystical experiences; sometimes they are found through drugs; and they are part of many religious traditions.

People who live in prosperity can devote time to their growth and development and can progress to a point where their lower needs are met. Then there is a possibility to move up to levels that involve having experiences that teach them about spirituality and the Infinite. Maslow posited that this our biological destiny, and a life force that drives us.

I Never Saw Such Eyes

I never saw such eyes as he had: soft, velvety, bleeding with impersonal love. When you passed Videha in the walkway, he was not like the rest of us, happily anxious to connect with a friendly face. No, Videha kept his eyes to himself.

When I lived in India for a year, one of the disciplines I practiced was Sufi whirling, the powerful method of remembrance of God danced by the whirling dervishes. Through it, I learned a tremendous amount, about life, about balance, and the nature of the Universe. Videha was our teacher, our Sufi Master.

Small boned, with long hair and beard, he was handsome but anonymously so, drawing no attention to himself or his looks. He always wore a slight smile, radiating quiet kindness. Videha wouldn't meet your eye when you walked by because he wasn't looking and thus didn't see you. It wasn't that he was spaced out or unfriendly, it was just a different kind of awareness than the rest of us "hungry ghosts."

The eyes, he taught us, are aggressive. Rather than take his word for it, I experimented and became aware of how my eyes attacked my environment, hungry for stimulation, for connection, for beauty. We talk about a "penetrating gaze." I

237

also saw that the eyes scan for things to criticize, to feel superior to. With the usual way of looking, the ego is in the driver seat, and there is violence in it.

A receptive eye, on the other hand, relaxes and receives impressions. It is soft, fluid, not judging or dividing. What is seen comes to it, rather than the eye going out to capture. This gaze is of that most denigrated concept in the West: passive.

Try it yourself: for a moment, look at something with your normal reaching-out and grasping eye. Inspect the object; take its measure. Then, practice relaxing your focus and contemplating with your receptive eye, receiving information about the object of your gaze, rather than dissecting it to divulge its secrets.

Imagine walking about in your world as Videha does, being a part of the environment but not the center of it, receiving information from people and things rather than "penetrating" them. How much less effort and striving would be involved? Which of these "eyes" do you think is more likely to receive love?

The point is not to lose the ability to reach out into our environment, but to become aware that it is not the only way to approach our lives and each other. Perhaps a discipline could be cultivated of exercising your receptive eye at times, to find out how much it could teach you.

Interview with the Swami

Swami Premodaya is a Los Angeles-based spiritual teacher who is unique in that before he began his current calling, he worked in the psychological field. For years, he headed hospital-based psychiatric programs, as well as working independently as a psychotherapist. I asked him about the relationship between psychology and spirituality:

"The simplest way to state it is that there's a divinely given responsibility to grow, to become really who you are, to blossom into your true potential. For the small minority of people who consciously hold that purposeful intention, it becomes imperative to grow psychologically because that's the base of growing in every other way. If you're psychologically impaired or immature, your ability to advance spiritually is limited."

How would that translate to practical advice? I asked.

"I recommend to your readers that if they want spiritual growth, they identify very clearly in what area of life they are out of balance. Life contains many required areas: work, social life, friendships, leisure time, finances, romantic relationships, health. Most people have areas of life that haven't been dealt with and are not functioning adequately, and these become barriers to growth. For example, if someone has a chaotic financial life, they're not going to be able to have the spiritual life they want or advance as far or as fast as they might like when they are constantly thrown back to deal with their money issues."

The way I say it is so that these areas don't capture your attention. Would he agree with that?

"Yes," Premodaya continued. "It's not required that you represent a pinnacle of health in every area of life, or that you be the best or perfect. It is required that your functioning is minimally adequate, so that each area is not a problem that becomes a crisis again and again.

"Competent outside help is often needed as it can't be done on your own or with the help of friends or family. People come to me for spiritual help and often the first thing I do is send them for psychological help because that will be the right order of things.

"For me, psychology is the beginning phase of spirituality. For those who seek spirituality, psychology is the entry point. I don't have a strong dividing line between the two—I tend to see it more as the rungs of a ladder. The top rung of the ladder of psychology is the bottom rung of the ladder of spirituality."

I often work with spiritual seekers needing psychological help, so I was happy to find out that the swami considers psychotherapy helpful. To learn more about Premodaya, visit www.premodaya.com.

Spiritual Emergency

I got a call earlier this week from a couple trying to get help for a beloved friend who was unable to get off the couch due to experiencing visions, flashes of color and light, sensations of energy coming out of her body, and ecstatic trance states. She also believes that the Messiah has returned, and it is she.

The couple had found me through Google as a "transpersonal" therapist, or one who has had training in assessing and treating what is called "spiritual emergency." For although their friend has a history of severe mental illness, many of her symptoms are the same or similar as those of spiritual awakening.

She was also experiencing evidence of a broader spiritual understanding, of increased compassion, of expansiveness, of the knowledge that everything is made of swirling energy, and that she has an important role to play on earth. Unfortunately, since this was mixed up with her psychotic symptoms, her friends weren't sure what to do.

They didn't want her to be just medicated and thrown into the hospital again. Conventionally trained mental health professionals are not taught how to distinguish between mental illness and spiritual awakening, which can at times resemble a psychotic break. Since Freud, there has been a bias against spirituality in mainstream psychology, and so, many people are understandably reluctant to seek the treatment they need.

Their friend was long ago diagnosed with bipolar disorder, and her mother had suffered from schizophrenia. The friend had been hospitalized for her illness in the past, gotten on medication, and improved significantly. Like many people, she went off the meds that were helping her so much due to side effects, and because she believed she didn't need them anymore. But something else of great import was happening also.

One of the things I learned in graduate school that has been a useful rule of thumb is that the mentally ill person is drowning in the sea while the mystic is treading water. They are both in the same sea, however. One of the ways we distinguish between the two states is to assess how stable the person has been able to be in their life—have they been able to care for their activities of daily living, provide shelter and food for themselves, for example.

As I said to the concerned couple on the phone, we need to first do a full assessment, then treat the mental illness and support the spiritual awakening.

It is important to find a therapist with special training in Spiritual Emergency. If you are not in the LA Area, you can locate one through the Professional Directory on the website for the Association for Transpersonal Psychology.

The Best Experience You've Ever Had

You've hiked to the top of the hill, and the vista spread out before you is breathtaking. Full of endorphins, you're overcome with a speechless appreciation of beauty. You suddenly know without a doubt that all is right with the world and your place in it, and you're in touch with a magnificence beyond your finite self. The moment changes you forever. Some people call this an experience of God; transpersonal psychologists call it a Peak Experience.

According to research conducted by Robert Wuthnow in the 1970s, 84% of the 1,000 people interviewed responded affirmatively to the questions: "Have you ever had the feeling that you were in close contact with something holy or sacred?" or "Have you experienced the beauty of nature in a deeply moving way?" or "Have you had the feeling that you were in harmony with the universe?" We can thus assume that most people we meet are familiar with an intense, emotional experience that put them in touch with something greater than themselves, was hard to put into words, and has had a profound effect on their life.

Peak experiences can come from a deep experience of nature as above, or through drugs, sex, meditation, or even when we are turned on by learning, as Gad Yair from Hebrew

University found out in research in 2009, in "singular, short and intense educational encounters that proved to have strong and long lasting results."

Earlier cultures understood the transformative possibilities of peak experiences and developed technologies to produce them: ecstatic practices such as drumming, dance, prayer, singing, ritual, drugs, Sufi whirling. Many of these techniques were introduced into mainstream Western culture in the latter part of the last millennium. Although he is most known as a an avid proponent of LSD, Dr. Timothy Leary importantly theorized that since a peak experience by its very definition changes us, in those peak moments we can change our conditioning to see the world in a more useful way. Group and individual psychotherapies have since been developed to facilitate the purposeful change of worldview for suffering people, especially addicts and those with PTSD.

Once you've had a peak (also referred to as transcendent, or spiritual) experience, you never view mainstream reality in the same way again. You've had a taste that more is available than you've been taught. Peak experiences are so full of promise, so enticing, that once you've had one, your whole life may become an effort to experience it again. However one comes, whether spontaneously or induced, a peak experience is always a great teacher and a boundless blessing.

The Prejudice Against Gurus

It's true there are charlatans and egomaniacs in the guru biz. The media delights in dramatic stories of crazed followers doing odd and dangerous things, like that guy who had everyone drink the purple Kool-Aid, or those folks who committed mass suicide while wearing brand new Nikes when the Hale-Bopp comet whizzed by. We shake our heads at such ignorance and smugly reject the notion that people surrender themselves to anything at all.

In the West, we're prejudiced against gurus. Here, ego reigns supreme, and the ego's first tenet is "nobody knows better than me." Granted, there's a lot to be said for how Americans distrust authority, question pomposity, and demand to ferret out the truth for ourselves. But by our closed-mindedness, we miss knowing about higher states of consciousness known to the East that aren't necessarily promoted on our nightly menu of sexy sitcoms and reality TV.

I got broken open to all this by amazing human beings I met in India. Although I had been studying personal and spiritual growth for decades, nothing had prepared me for the shock of the energy phenomena in their presence. It was as if I had taken psychedelic drugs when I hadn't: the room began to swirl, the lights bending and warping. My breathing changed as it does when you're having sex—gasping for air, tingling all over. My mind became blessedly silent—everything okay, perfect just the way it is.

Okay, maybe you're thinking it was something I ate, or a weird brain fugue or something. I can only explain it as these persons manifest at a higher frequency than we do, that in their presence, our bodies go haywire. It became irrefutable that there's more going on than Western culture has given us a context for, and that higher levels of human development exist and are available.

The tradition in the East is to surrender to the Guru, and the media is quick to point out abuses. What isn't shown is the advantage of surrendering one's belief that "I already knows everything, and no one can teach me anything." The benefit is immeasurable in one's becoming teachable, the ego humbling itself in the presence of something so far beyond it.

In the East, it's believed that the Guru points the Way. We get confused because we think it's about following another person's weird dictates, such as "Give me all your money" or "Drink this potion." Osho, a well-known guru, once explained it by saying, "Don't look at my finger; look where I'm pointing."

My experience is that absorbing the radiance of a person of higher frequency is in itself uplifting and healing. Sitting in the presence of an Awakened Being will do more for your spiritual growth than years of working on yourself.

Women of High Spiritual Attainment

Today we are blessed with a plethora of contemporary women spiritual teachers: Marianne Williamson, Pema Chodron, Gangaji, Gurumayi, Ammachi, Sylvia Boorstein and her many Buddhist colleagues. Accredited graduate programs in Women's Spirituality have opened, and everywhere women are being ordained as ministers and rabbis.

Such abundance wasn't available when I started on my spiritual path. All the persons of spiritual attainment to study or emulate were men. In fact, many teachers declared that women cannot become enlightened, that we will have to wait to be reborn as men. The so-called "perennial philosophy" and Ken Wilbur's interpretations privileged male ways of being and worshiping, while placing non-rational, emotional, and intuitive spiritual paths at the bottom of their hierarchies.

Over the years, I've researched women for whom spirituality was the central core of their lives. Here are a few you might find inspiring:

- **Alexandra David-Neal:** The first Westerner to be allowed to enter Tibet, she traveled for years in search of spiritual knowledge and experience, had a great tantric love affair with the king of Sikkim, and was still writing books about her adventures at the age of 100.

- **Hildegard von Bingen:** A nun and mystic whose music is still selling well on Amazon. A great scholar, writer, composer, scientist, and founder of monasteries. Although she lived in medieval times, she could truly be considered a "Renaissance woman" for the breadth of her knowledge and talents.

- **Irina Tweedie:** A Sufi teacher and author of *Daughter of Fire*, a journal of her intense spiritual journey. (Inadvertently surprising to read because she wrote it in her 50s—considered "elderly" only a few decades ago.)

- **Mary:** In Sunday school I was taught to see Mary as a passive vessel merely impregnated by the Holy Spirit. According to esoteric literature, however, she was a scholar and temple priestess. Mary had been identified early as the future mother of the Messiah, and was thus initiated as a young child and prepared and educated for the great task ahead.

- **St Theresa of Avila:** 16th century ecstatic mystic, theologian, and reformer of the Carmelite order of nuns. Her autobiography is one of the great classics of spiritual literature.

- **Lady Tsogyal:** 8th Century Tibetan Buddhist saint, Queen, and consort of the great tantric teacher, Padmasambhava. Her enlightenment was stated to be as high as that of any Buddha.

I encourage you to find out more about these wonderful ladies' lives. It's exciting and inspirational to learn about our foremothers of spiritual power and attainment.

Seven Signs that You are Making Spiritual Progress

A popular post circulating Facebook recently posited that the signs of spiritual progress are about becoming increasingly upbeat, positive, and blissful, a common New Age misconception. Spiritual progress is not about entering an eternally ecstatic state—that's called being high. Instead, you'll know real spiritual growth has occurred when you experience the following:

1) You welcome all your emotions.

Beginners on the spiritual path often believe that they must be positive all the time, criticizing themselves for having normal human feelings such as grief, jealousy, rage, negativity, or a just-plain bad day. You'll know you're progressing when you accept that all emotions are essential to the human experience. You wouldn't want to miss a second of what's true in the moment, instead of attempting to force yourself into being someone you're not.

2) You do the right thing without thinking about it.

When the cashier gives you the wrong change, you give it back without even considering whether or not it's the right thing to do. You've looked deeply into the issue and seen that doing the wrong thing creates static, self

249

recrimination, or negative repercussions, and it's gone deep within you to perform right action to the best of your ability.

3) You've successfully challenged your parents' and your culture's brainwashing, kept what works, and resoundingly rejected what doesn't.

People often do not understand the depth of their brainwashing. It's shocking to see how mechanical you and others are, going along with the program. Of course, many of the things you learned from your parents and culture are good and useful, and you want to keep those. But messages about sexuality, race, entertainment, and what is of value in life are things you will want to question and, in many cases, reject the prevailing notions.

4) You have increasing compassion for yourself and others.

You've begun to discover that everyone is in pain, including celebrities with their pseudo-perfect lives, the people on the street you've made fun of, and yourself. You understand that we're all in this human predicament together and are developing a soft, empathic response to it.

5) You've done your inner work.

Everyone has psychological digging to do, and you're committed to seeing it to completion. If there are still places inside yourself where you're afraid to go, you're not done yet. Do this work with a competent therapist who understands your spiritual longings.

6) You've embraced your humanity.

You've given up the dream of becoming super human,

immortal, mega-rich, or having the perfect body. You've decided to live here on planet earth with the rest of us imperfect folks who are just like you.

7) You agree with life.

You've given up your rose-colored glasses and accepted that life is challenging and will never become a Garden of Eden. You understand that much of life is suffering, and that you will continue to experience heartbreak for the rest of your life. You've accepted aging and death as a great adventure. You agree with who you are, who you've been, and the fact that you will be leaving here shortly. Amen.

Mind the Gap

I visited my sister and her family during the year in London her husband pursued graduate work in play directing. My nephews hated British school, their American ways considered freakish and weird by the other kids. It was hard to eat well, as the produce offered in the grocery stores was at least a week old, but I loved visiting the places I'd dreamed of: Buckingham Palace, the Tate Modern, wherever it was the Bloomsbury crowd hung out, and Carnaby Street, the center of 60s fashion. I cried at Poet's Corner in Westminster Abbey seeing the memorials of Chaucer, Blake, Keats, and other great literary figures, comparing the reverence paid to that of American popular culture which considers poets just above the level of dirt.

We took the Underground everywhere, also known as the Tube, London's clean and efficient rapid transit system. The Tube was great for people watching—nearly everyone looked puffy and as if they didn't eat many fresh vegetables. There were signs posted all over that said *Mind the Gap*—a safety reminder for people to watch their step as they traversed from the platform to the train.

It seemed a bit more metaphysical to me.

Buddhists practice a meditation of watching the breath. It can be quite powerful to sit and observe the long inhale as it draws in, chest and lungs expanding, hopefully the abdomen and belly, too. Then to watch the long exhale, with its calming effect. When you sit with the breath long enough, you may experience an eerie sensation that you are not breathing at all —something is breathing you. In fact, it seems more accurate to say we are being "breathed."

Osho, the great tantra master, however, said it's really about watching for the gap between the ingoing and outgoing breath. It takes a little awareness, but you can locate it if you slow way down, and if you look closely, you'll notice a space between each inhale and exhale where nothing is happening. There's a gap, a silence, a doorway to another reality. It's like the silence between words, the white space on the page, the background murmur rather than the foreground conversation. That's the gap, Osho said, where who you are really exists.

Another of my favorite memories of London was touring the Globe Theater, and our guide whose raucous stories split our sides with laughter. But the thing I loved most about London was these spiritual reminders appearing everywhere, all over underneath the town. Mind the Gap. Remember to find out who you really are.

Acknowledgments

Thanks to my friends and family, especially those who have encouraged my writing: Gary Bowsher, Kimberly Bowsher, Leslie Keenan, Mark Bizzell, Maureen T. Smith, Spencer Grendahl, Ziri Rideaux, and Dean Santomieri. Thanks to Calin Popescu and the "Defeat Procrastination Creative Writers' Club of LA."

Thanks to my patients and the readers of my blog and newsletter. I appreciate your feedback, questions, and questing spirits.

Thanks to my writing teachers, particularly Andy Courtier and Holly Prado Northup, who as well as teaching me to be a better writer, have acted as spiritual guides and mentors.

Thanks to my many teachers in life, most of all, beloved Osho.

About the Author

Catherine Auman, LMFT (Licensed Marriage and Family Therapist) is a spiritual psychotherapist and the Director of The Transpersonal Counseling Center in Los Angeles, California. She has advanced training in traditional psychology as well as the wisdom traditions. Catherine's writings have been published in journals, magazines, and books in the US, Finland, and Norway. She has a BA in Literature and a Certificate in Creative Writing from Berkeley City College.

Connect with Catherine Auman

Visit her **online** at www.catherineauman.com

Facebook: www.facebook.com/catherine.auman

LinkedIn: www.linkedin.com/in/catherineauman

Twitter: www.twitter.com/catherineauman

Google+: www.google.com/+CatherineAuman

Blog: www.catherineauman.com/blog/

Alphabetical Index

Made in the USA
San Bernardino, CA
30 July 2015